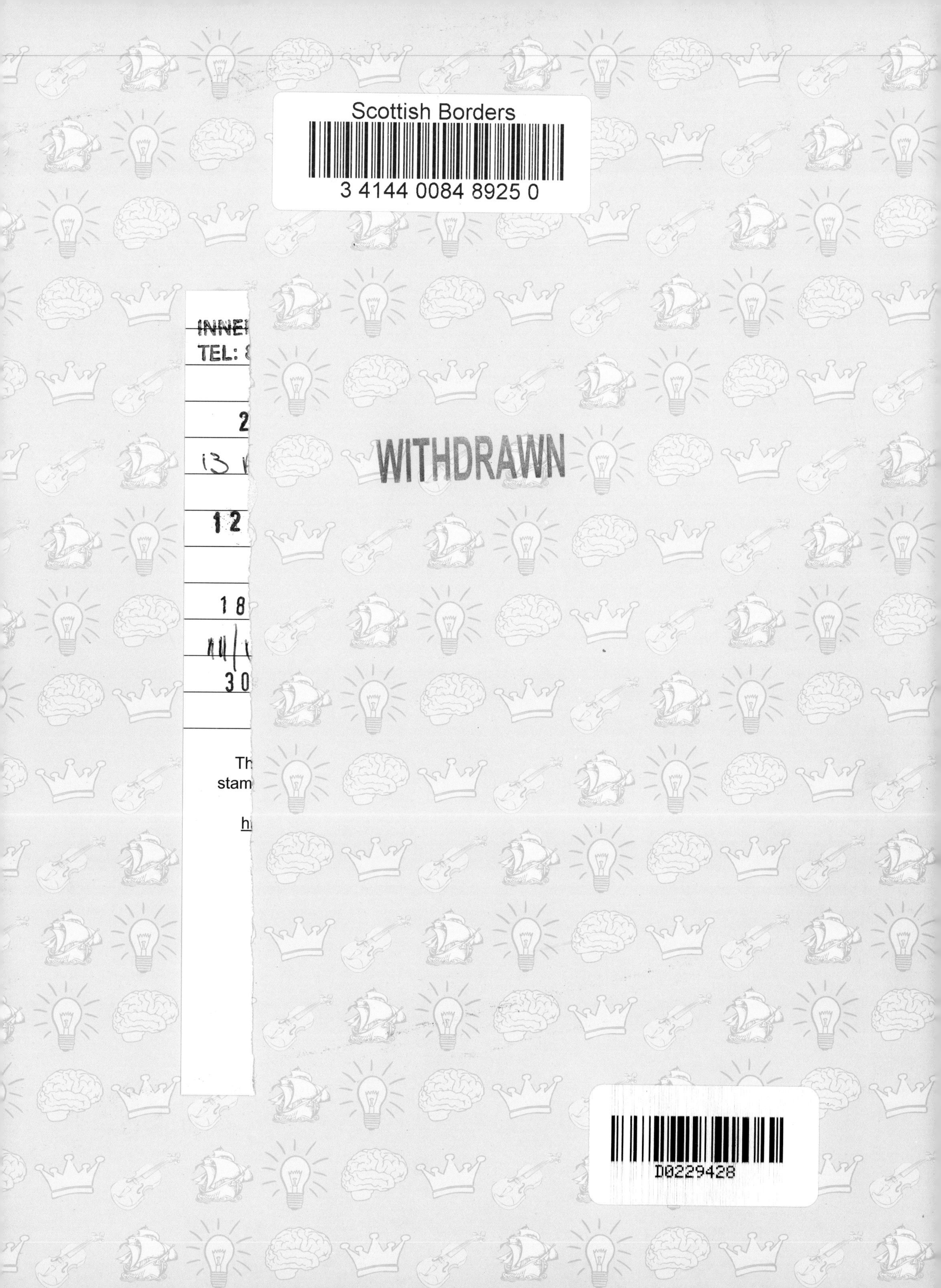

100
people
who made
history
Meet the people
who shaped the
modern world

London, New York, Melbourne, Munich, and Delhi

Senior editor Jenny Sich
Senior art editor Stefan Podhorodecki

Project editor Ashwin Khurana
Designer Hoa Luc

Editors Matilda Gollon, James Mitchem, Jessamy Wood
Additional designers Angela Ball, Dave Ball

Managing editor Linda Esposito
Managing art editor Diane Peyton Jones
Category publisher Laura Buller

Publishing director Jonathan Metcalf
Associate publishing director Liz Wheeler
Art director Phil Ormerod

Jacket editor Manisha Majithia
Jacket designer Yumiko Tahata
Design development manager Sophia M. Tampakopoulos Turner

Picture researcher Rob Nunn
DK picture librarian Romaine Werblow
Production editor John Goldsmid
Senior production controller Angela Graef

First published in Great Britain in 2012 by
Dorling Kindersley Limited,
80 Strand, London WC2R 0RL

2 4 6 8 10 9 7 5 3 1
001–182782 – Feb/12

A CIP catalogue for this book is available from the British Library.

ISBN: 978-1-40539-145-0

Hi-res workflow proofed by MDP, UK
Printed and bound by Hung Hing, Hong Kong, China

Discover more at
www.dk.com

Written by Ben Gilliland

Consultant Philip Parker

Contents

Daring

Discoverers

There are adventurous discoverers who boldy go where no one has gone before, sailing the high seas and finding new lands. Then there are the more stay-at-home types, who toil away in labs and the like and – eureka – discover something that will save millions of lives. Behind every great discovery is a remarkable person, whose courage and determination – and sometimes plain luck – made the world the place it is today.

All about me

- **BORN:** 1254
- **DIED:** 1324
- **NATIONALITY:** Italian
- **FACTOID:** I travelled more than 4,000 km (14,900 miles).
- **IN A NUTSHELL:** My father and uncle travelled to China to trade jewels and met the Mongol ruler.

By the way...
my book gave Europe its first look into Asia, but many people didn't believe me and said I'd made it up.

Marco Polo

The man whose journey of a lifetime brought the FAR EAST to Europe

Marco sets off

When Marco was 17, he accompanied his father and uncle when they **returned to China** (see purple line on map). They spent 17 years in the court of the Mongol ruler of China, ***Kublai Khan***. He really liked Marco, first making him a diplomat and then the **GOVERNOR** of the city of Yangzhou.

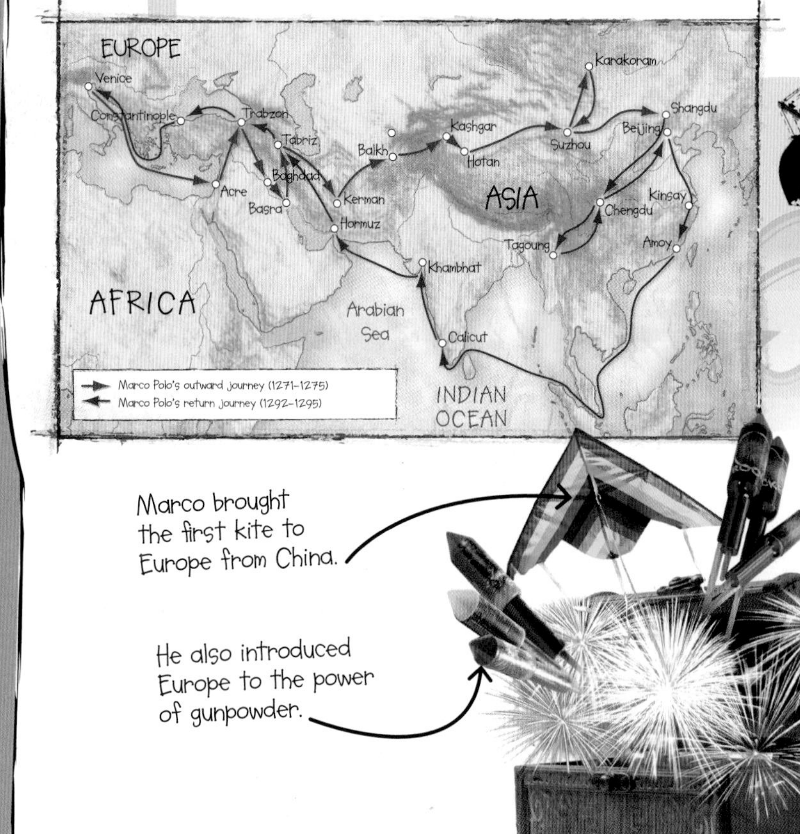

Return to Venice

Khan liked Marco so much that, even though the Polos asked to return home, he **refused to let them leave**. Luckily, in 1292, the Polos were sent to escort a Mongol princess to Persia (modern-day Iran). They seized the opportunity, **ESCAPED**, and returned home after 24 years (see pink line on map). Marco wrote a book about his adventures, ***The Travels of Marco Polo***.

All about me

- **BORN:** 1304
- **DIED:** 1368
- **NATIONALITY:** Moroccan
- **FACTOID:** My adventures took me more than 121,000 km (75,185 miles).
- **IN A NUTSHELL:** My family were rich scholars. At 21, I went on "hajj", a Muslim pilgrimage to Mecca (in modern-day Saudi Arabia), the holiest city in Islam.

Catching the travel bug

Battuta's journey to Mecca took him along the North African coast, through Egypt, and the Middle East (each colour on the map shows a different stage of his journey). Along the way, he was **ATTACKED BY BANDITS**, fell ill, and even got married. Even though it took him ***16 months to reach Mecca***, he decided he hadn't done enough travelling, so he set off for **more adventures**.

Country hopping

Battuta travelled to Mesopotamia (modern-day Iraq), and then to Persia (Iran), before returning to Mecca, where he spent **a year recovering from diarrhoea**. Over the next **26 YEARS**, he travelled to India, Anatolia, the Black Sea, the Caspian Sea, Afghanistan, China, and Timbuktu. ***When he finally got home***, in 1354, he wrote a book, the *Rihla,* which means "The Journey" in Arabic.

By the way... I never travelled the same route twice, except to Mecca. When I wrote my book, many people thought my adventures couldn't be true.

Ibn Battuta

The Islamic scholar who just couldn't stop TRAVELLING

Christopher Columbus

The EXPLORER who stumbled across the New World

Christopher Columbus is known as "the man who discovered America", even though he didn't really know what he had discovered!

Wind in his sails

Christopher Columbus was born in 1451 in Genoa, Italy. He was **just a teenager** when he was first sent to sea, and after lots of travelling he made Portugal his home. Intrigued by the ***spices and gold*** on offer in the parts of the Far East, Columbus believed that he could find a quicker sea route to reach there. So at a time when most explorers sailed east towards the Far East, Columbus came up with a plan to search for it by **SAILING WEST**.

Columbus took three ships on the voyage – the *Santa Maria*, the *Pinta*, and the *Niña*.

He couldn't have done it without...

The remarkable adventures of **Marco Polo** *(1254–1324) in China helped to open up valuable trade routes to the Far East.*

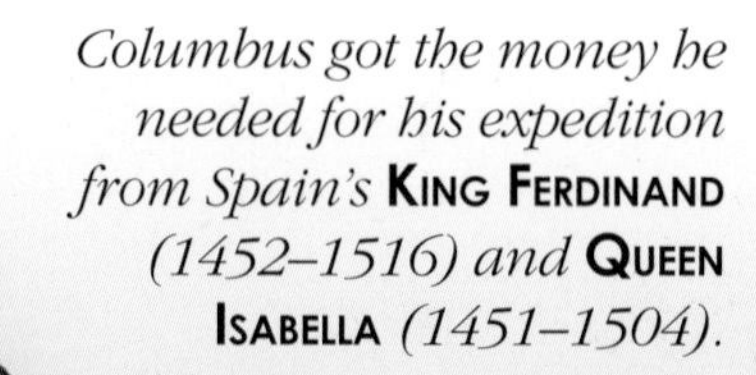

Columbus got the money he needed for his expedition from Spain's **King Ferdinand** *(1452–1516) and* **Queen Isabella** *(1451–1504).*

Accidental hero

After being turned down in Portugal, Columbus got the funding he needed from Spain and, in 1492, he set sail across the **Atlantic Ocean**. Ten weeks later, his ships spotted land and Columbus went ashore on what he thought was an island near India, calling the indigenous people "Indians" – he was actually in the Caribbean. Of course, Columbus hadn't found a ***shortcut to India***, but he did discover the land we would come to know as **AMERICA**.

By the way...
I was not the first European to reach the Americas. It was actually discovered 500 years earlier by a Viking called Leif Eriksson.

Columbus used the position of the stars, the Moon, and the Sun to find his way at sea.

Age of empires

The discovery of America by Columbus started centuries of conquest and colonization that changed the world forever. However, as countries built up their empires, many indigenous people suffered.

He paved the way for...

Although he died along the way, in 1519, the Portuguese explorer **Ferdinand Magellan** *(1480–1521) led the first crew ever to sail around the world.*

Another Portuguese explorer, **Vasco da Gama** *(c.1460–1524), was the first to sail directly from Europe to India.*

Galileo Galilei

The "father of MODERN science"

By the way... the moons of Jupiter are known as the Galilean moons and the first spacecraft to orbit Jupiter was named after me, too.

Galileo was an astronomer, physicist, mathematician, and inventor. He is considered to be one of the most famous scientists of all time.

From medicine to maths

Galileo Galilei was born in 1564 near Pisa, Italy. He ***studied medicine*** at the University of Pisa, but changed his mind and switched to **mathematics**, and, in 1589, he became a professor of mathematics. In 1609, Galileo heard about something called a **TELESCOPE** that had been invented in Holland.

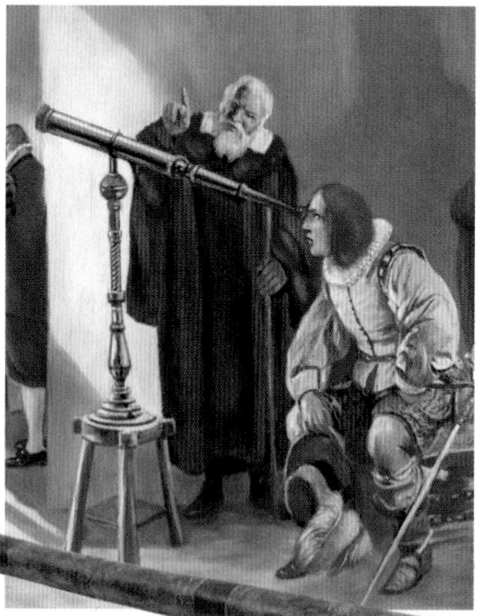

I spy with my little eye

Amazingly, even though Galileo had never seen a telescope, he **BUILT HIS OWN VERSION** that was much better than the original. Using his new telescope, he discovered mountains and valleys on the surface of the Moon, **sunspots**, and the moons of Jupiter. His discoveries made him a ***celebrity***.

Galileo originally sold his telescope as a way for towns to spot approaching enemy ships.

He couldn't have done it without...

The great **ARCHIMEDES** *(c.287–212 BCE) was one of the first people to suggest that the* **EARTH ORBITS THE SUN**.

PTOLEMY *(90–168 CE) created* **ASTRONOMICAL TABLES** *that allowed people to calculate the location of the planets.*

Galileo versus God

In one of his books, Galileo explained how the Earth orbits the Sun. The church didn't like this because it taught that the Earth is the **centre of the Universe**. In 1616, Galileo was accused of ***heresy*** and forbidden from teaching or talking about his theories. He didn't obey the church's request for long, and, in 1633, he was sentenced to **LIFE IN PRISON** unless he renounced his beliefs.

It might seem silly to us, but before Galileo most people believed that the Sun and the planets orbited the Earth.

Saturn
Venus
Earth
Sun
Jupiter
Mercury
Moon
Mars

Did you know?
Galileo didn't get everything right. He thought that the tides were caused by oceans sloshing about as Earth orbits the Sun.

Falling for gravity

Galileo performed lots of different **experiments**. He proved that heavy and light objects **FALL AT THE SAME SPEED** and how gravity makes falling objects ***accelerate***. He also worked out that the only thing that affects how fast a pendulum swings (like the ones you find in some old clocks) is its length and the strength of gravity.

leo dropped different nonballs from Tower of Pisa prove that ects fall at same speed.

Trailblazer
Albert Einstein called Galileo the "father of modern science". His discoveries undermined the power of the church and helped give scientists the freedom to talk about their work without fear of persecution.

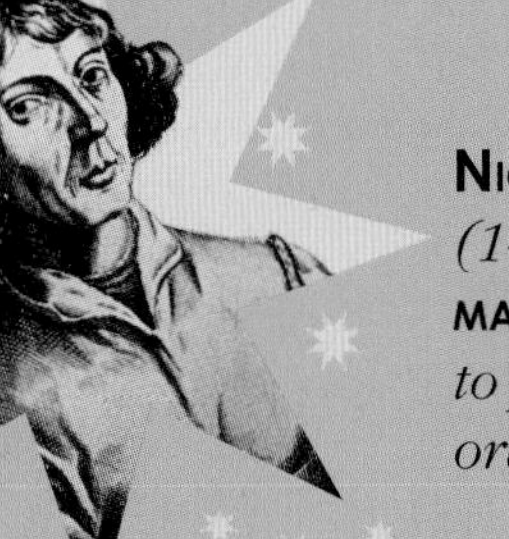

NICOLAS COPERNICUS *(1473–1543) used* **MATHEMATICAL MODELS** *to prove that the Earth orbits the Sun.*

The nobleman **TYCHO BRAHE** *(1546–1601) made the most accurate* **ASTRONOMICAL MEASUREMENTS** *of his day.*

Isaac Newton

The man who got HEAVY with gravity

Isaac Newton figured out why objects fall to the ground and why the planets move the way they do.

Plagued with questions

Isaac Newton was born in Lincolnshire, England, in 1643. His father died before he was born but, despite having a difficult childhood, he gained a place at **Cambridge University.** When the **PLAGUE** broke out he was forced home and, with so much free time on his hands, Newton started to wonder about ***what made things fall***.

An apple a day

Newton said that he was inspired to think about forces when he saw an ***apple fall from a tree***. He came up with the theory of **GRAVITY**, an invisible force that **pulls all of the objects** in the Universe together, and the reason things don't float off into the sky.

By the way...
I made most of my discoveries between the ages of 21 and 27, but didn't publish many of them until years later.

He couldn't have done it without...

The German astronomer JOHANNES KEPLER'S *(1571–1630)* LAWS OF PLANETARY MOTION *showed how planets orbit the Sun.*

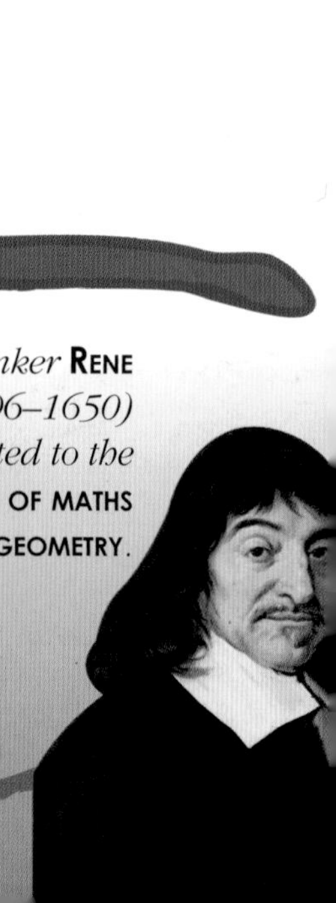

The French thinker RENE DESCARTES *(1596–1650) contributed to the* DEVELOPMENT OF MATHS AND GEOMETRY.

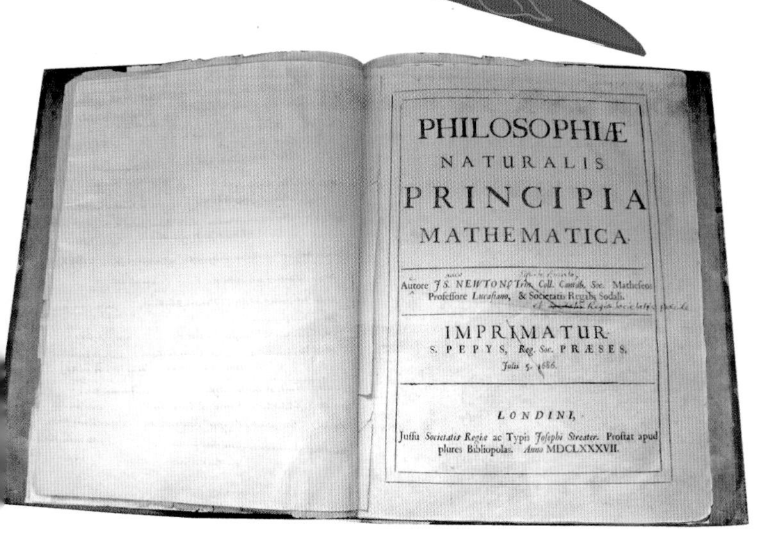
PHILOSOPHIÆ
NATURALIS
PRINCIPIA
MATHEMATICA.

Autore J S. NEWTON, Trin. Coll. Cantab. Soc. Matheseos Professore Lucasiano, & Societatis Regalis Sodali.

IMPRIMATUR.
S. PEPYS, Reg. Soc. PRÆSES.
Julii 5. 1686.

LONDINI,
Jussu Societatis Regiæ ac Typis Josephi Streater. Prostat apud plures Bibliopolas. Anno MDCLXXXVII.

Laying down the law

In 1685, Newton described his **LAWS OF MOTION** – a mathematical guide to how an object's movement is affected by **speed and mass**. Two years later, Newton published his ideas about gravity in his book, ***Philosophiae Naturalis Principia Mathematica***, which contains many of the foundations of modern science.

Newton showed how gravity affects the orbits of planets.

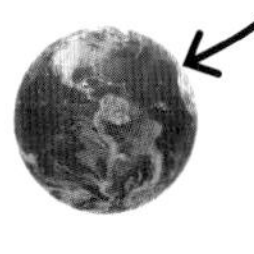

One of the greatest

Newton's work on gravity and motion revolutionized science for more than 200 years, and gave us a new understanding about how the Earth and Universe work. When he died in 1727, Newton was buried among royalty at Westminster Abbey, London, UK.

Light fantastic

Newton also invented a new kind of telescope called a **REFLECTOR**. It used a mirror to collect light instead of lenses, and was **much more powerful than existing telescopes**. He also showed that white light was made up of ***all the colours of the rainbow***.

Newton used a glass prism to split light into separate colours.

He paved the way for...

Astronomers used Newton's laws to find **URANUS, NEPTUNE, AND THE DWARF PLANET PLUTO,** *which they couldn't find without his telescope.*

The **HUBBLE SPACE TELESCOPE** *is based on Newton's reflecting telescope design, called a Newtonian telescope.*

Dmitri Mendeleev

The man who brought the ELEMENTS to the table

Dmitri Mendeleev revolutionized chemistry when he created the first version of the periodic table of elements.

> **By the way...**
> I was nominated for the Nobel Prize in Chemistry in 1906, but I didn't get it because my discovery was too old by then.

Elementary student

Born in 1834 in Tobolsk, Russia, Mendeleev studied science in St Petersburg and became a **professor of chemistry**. As a teacher, he thought that if he could organize the chemical elements, it would ***help his students*** to understand them. This was a difficult task, and he spent years trying to figure out how to do it.

PERIODIC TABLE

1 H Hydrogen 1.0							
3 6.9	4 Be						
11 Na Sodium 23.0	12 Mg Magnesium 24.3						
19 K Potassium 39.1	20 Ca Calcium 40.1	21 Sc Scandium 45.0	22 Ti Titanium 47.9	23 V Vanadium 50.9	Cr Chromium 52.0	25 54.9	26
37 Rb Rubidium 85.5	38 Sr Strontium 87.6	39 Y Yttrium 88.9	40 Zr Zirconium 91.2	41 Nb Niobium 92.9	42 Mo Molybdenum 95.9	43 Tc Technetium 99	Ru Rutheni 101.0
55 Cs Caesium 132.9	56 Ba Barium 137.3	57-71 See below	72 Hf Hafnium 178.5	73 Ta Tantalum 180.9	74 W Tungsten 183.9	75 Re Rhenium 186.2	76 Os Osmiu 190.2
87 Fr Francium 223.0	88 Ra Radium 226.0	89-103 See below	104 Unq Unnilquadium 261	105 Unp Unnilpentium 262	106 Unh Unnilhexium 263	107 Uns Unnilseptium 262	108 Unc Unniloct 265

57 La Lanthanum 138.9	58 Ce Cerium 140.1	59 Pr Praseodymium 140.9	60 Nd Neodymium 144.2	61 Pm Promethium 145	62 Sm Samariu 150.4
89 Ac Actinium 227.0	90 Th Thorium 232.0	91 Pa Protactinium 231.0	92 U Uranium 238.0	93 Np Neptunium 237	94 Pu Plutoniu 242

The vertical columns are called groups, which contain elements with similar properties.

Each family is a different colour.

The horizontal rows (periods) correspond with the number of electrons (negatively charged particles) that orbit the nucleus. So, hydrogen in row 1 has one electron and barium in row 6 has six.

87 Fr Francium 223.0

Atomic number is the total number of protons (positively charged particles) in the nucleus

Chemical symbol is shorthand for the element

Name of the periodic element

Atomic mass gives the number of protons and neutrons (particles without an electric charge) in the nucleus

He couldn't have done it without...

The Greek philosopher **Democritus** *(460–370 BCE) suggested that everything was made up of atoms, which means "indivisible" in Greek.*

Robert Boyle *(1627–1691) was an Irish chemist who was able to prove that gases are made up of widely spaced, moving atoms.*

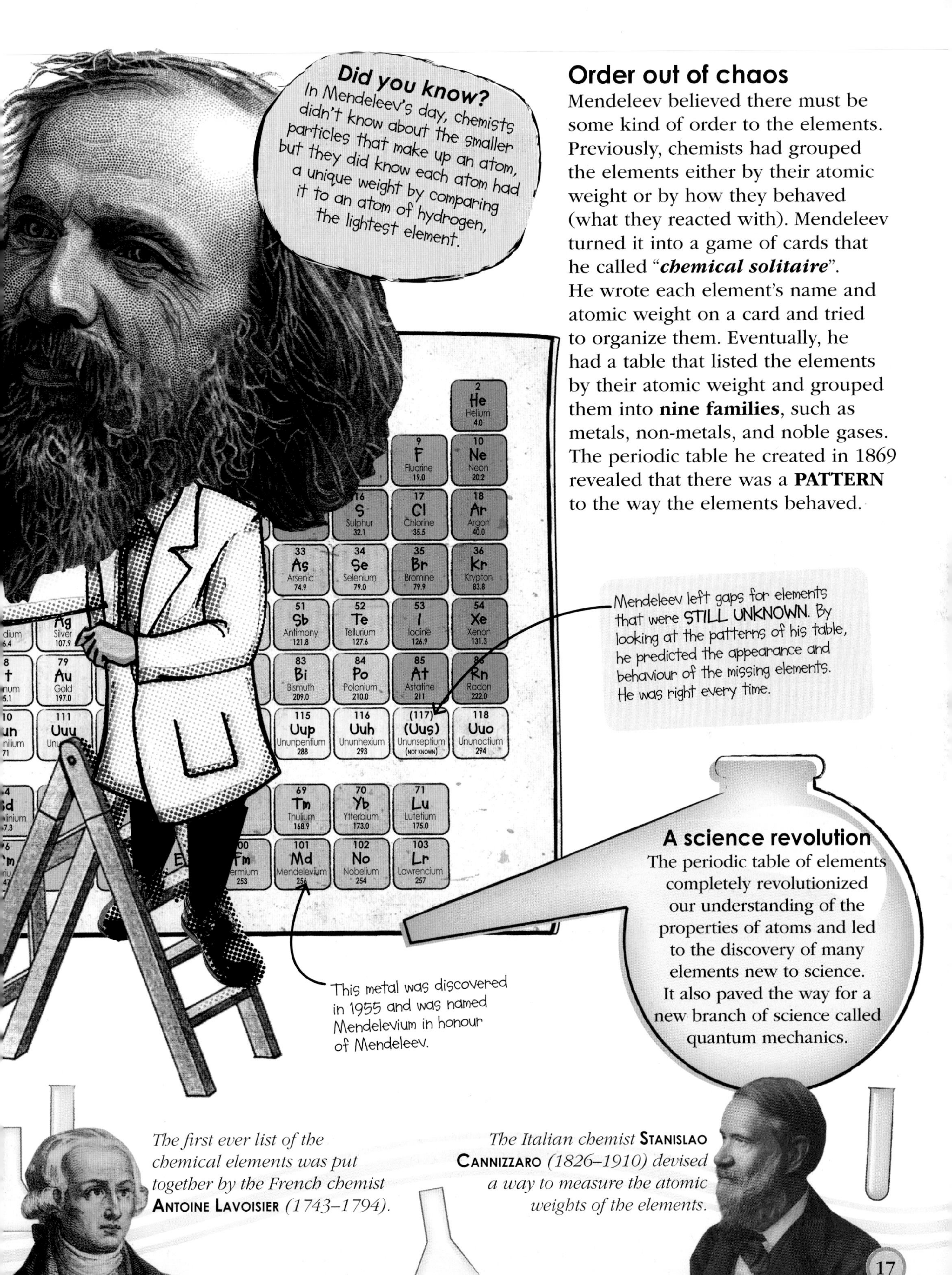

Order out of chaos

Mendeleev believed there must be some kind of order to the elements. Previously, chemists had grouped the elements either by their atomic weight or by how they behaved (what they reacted with). Mendeleev turned it into a game of cards that he called "***chemical solitaire***". He wrote each element's name and atomic weight on a card and tried to organize them. Eventually, he had a table that listed the elements by their atomic weight and grouped them into **nine families**, such as metals, non-metals, and noble gases. The periodic table he created in 1869 revealed that there was a **PATTERN** to the way the elements behaved.

A science revolution

The periodic table of elements completely revolutionized our understanding of the properties of atoms and led to the discovery of many elements new to science. It also paved the way for a new branch of science called quantum mechanics.

The first ever list of the chemical elements was put together by the French chemist **ANTOINE LAVOISIER** *(1743–1794).*

The Italian chemist **STANISLAO CANNIZZARO** *(1826–1910) devised a way to measure the atomic weights of the elements.*

Charles Darwin

Making a MONKEY of mankind

Darwin showed that the complexity of life on Earth is the result of millions of years of gradual change and not of a single act of biblical creation.

Early years

Charles Darwin was born into a wealthy family in Shrewsbury, England, in 1809. As a young man Darwin wanted to be a **doctor**, but he ***hated*** the sight of blood, so he studied religion instead. He learned about **Natural Theology**, which taught how God designed life on Earth… but he would soon question this idea.

An incredible voyage

When he was just 22, Darwin joined a scientific expedition on a ship called HMS *Beagle*. He spent the five-year voyage ***observing nature***, which included making notes and collecting samples. While visiting the **GALÁPAGOS ISLANDS** in the Pacific Ocean, Darwin noticed that animals that were obviously related looked slightly different on different islands.

The finches that started Darwin thinking have become a symbol for evolution.

He couldn't have done it without…

Swedish botanist **CARL LINNAEUS** *(1707–1778) came up with the modern way of grouping related species together, also known as* **TAXONOMY**.

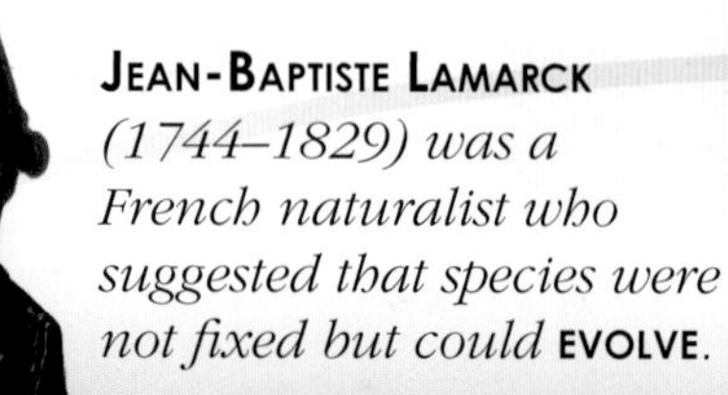

JEAN-BAPTISTE LAMARCK *(1744–1829) was a French naturalist who suggested that species were not fixed but could* **EVOLVE**.

By the way... lots of people hated my theory because it suggested that humans had evolved, just like any other animal.

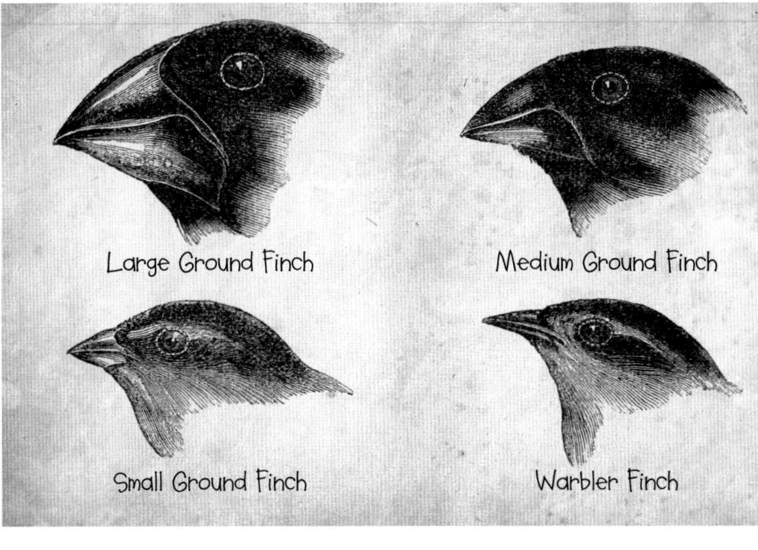

Natural Selection

Finches with large, strong beaks lived on islands with lots of seeds, but those on islands with lots of insects had narrow, pointy beaks. Darwin realized they had ***adapted*** to fit each island's unique environment. The animals with features best suited to where they lived were more likely to survive to pass on those features to their offspring. So, he had discovered that **SPECIES CHANGE** over a long period of time – he called this theory "**Evolution by the Process of Natural Selection**".

World-changing book

His book *On the Origin of Species* became an instant bestseller when it was published in 1859. Darwin's theory is one of the most important scientific ideas of all time. He changed the way we look at life on Earth forever.

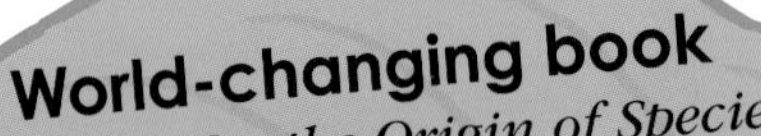

Darwin revolutionized the science of biology

Each island of the Galápagos has its own unique species of giant tortoise.

The English economist **Thomas Malthus** *(1766–1834) wrote about the* **struggle for existence** *in human populations, which influenced Darwin.*

British academic **Alfred Russel Wallace** *(1823–1913) sent his own* **theory of evolution** *to Darwin, spurring Darwin on to publish his own work.*

Medical marvels

The men who made MEDICINE modern

Not so long ago you were as likely to die from the treatment your doctor gave you as you were from the disease itself. These medical pioneers changed all that.

Did you know?
In Greece, Hippocrates (460–370 BCE) was the first person to say that diseases were not caused by evil spirits!

Edward Jenner
(1749–1823)

In the 18th century, ***smallpox*** – a contagious disease that causes a serious rash – was **England's biggest killer**. Jenner had the idea that if people were given a weak dose of smallpox, their body would be prepared to fight off a stronger infection. Jenner had invented a smallpox **VACCINATION**, which has been saving lives ever since.

Bacteria are still the world's biggest killer

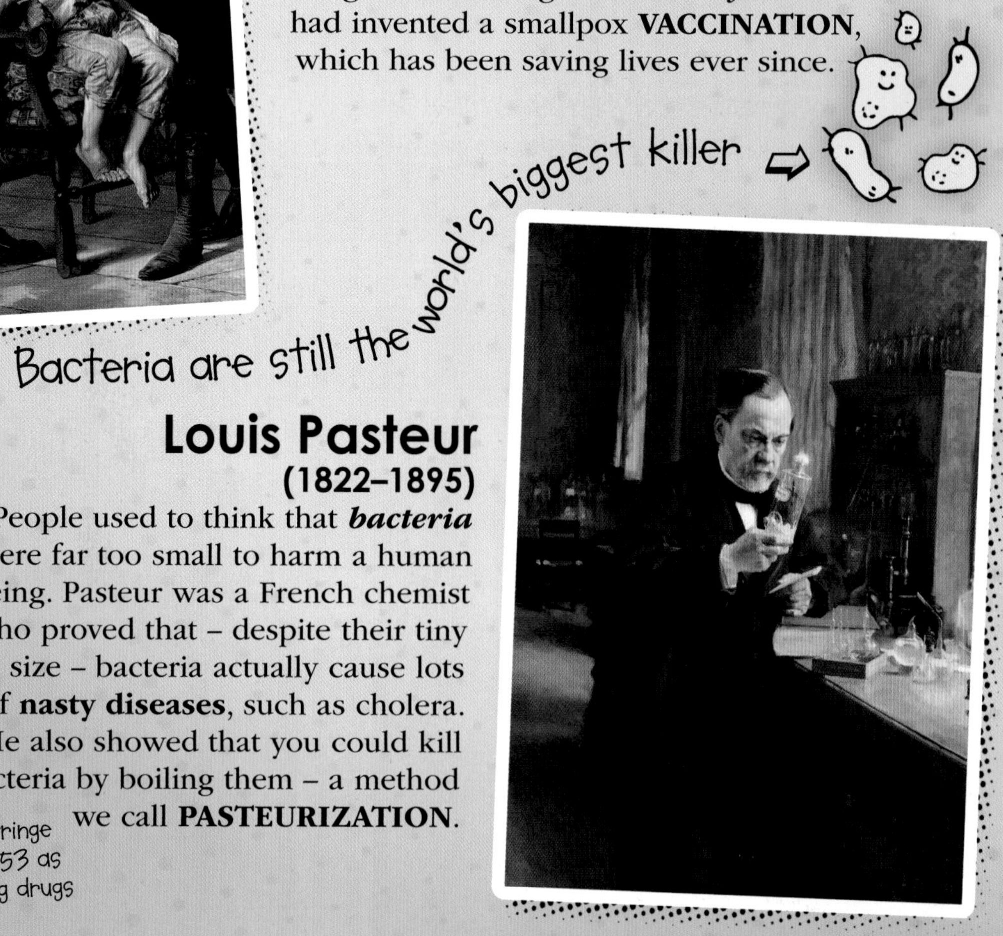

Louis Pasteur
(1822–1895)

People used to think that ***bacteria*** were far too small to harm a human being. Pasteur was a French chemist who proved that – despite their tiny size – bacteria actually cause lots of **nasty diseases**, such as cholera. He also showed that you could kill bacteria by boiling them – a method we call **PASTEURIZATION**.

The hypodermic syringe was invented in 1853 as a way of delivering drugs beneath the skin.

The earliest known surgery was performed as early as 10,000 BCE

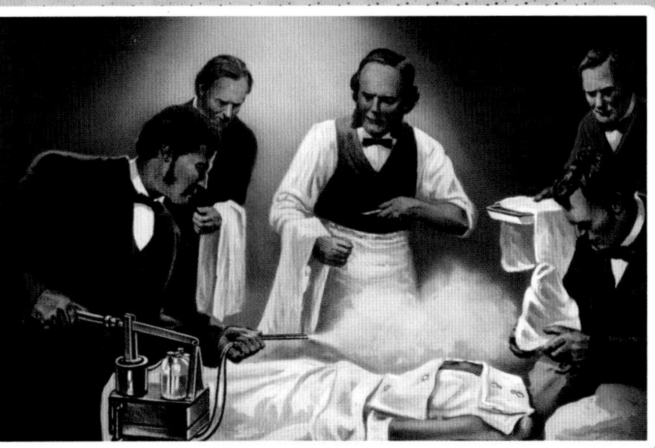

Joseph Lister
(1827–1912)

In the 19th century, lots of people died after surgery. Lister was a British doctor who believed that this was because ***germs*** from **dirty equipment** and unwashed hands were infecting patients during an operation. He came up with the idea of sterilizing equipment and treating wounds with **ANTISEPTICS**, substances that prevent the growth of disease-creating micro-organisms. Sterilization worked and, as a result, less people died after surgery.

Wilhelm Roentgen
(1845–1923)

When the German physicist Wilhelm Roentgen was experimenting with passing electric currents through gases, he noticed something **very strange**. He had produced a mysterious form of radiation that seemed to pass through objects. Uncertain with what he was dealing with, he called his discovery **X-RAYS**. Today, X-rays are used in medicine to ***detect*** everything from broken bones to various forms of cancer.

Alexander Fleming
(1881–1955)

This Scottish doctor was growing bacteria on petri dishes when he noticed that some dishes had grown **mouldy**. Before he threw out the dishes, he noticed that the mould seemed to have ***killed*** the bacteria he was growing. He called the substance **PENICILLIN**, and it was the very first antibiotic.

In 1816, the first stethoscope was made of rolled-up paper. Later it became a wooden tube.

His most famous equation showed that mass (m) and energy (E) are interchangeable. Even a tiny piece of matter (such as a pea) contains HUGE amounts of energy locked within its atoms. The energy in the object is the same as its mass times the speed of light (c), squared.

$E=mc^2$

Einstein is the world's most famous scientist. His theories changed forever the way we look at the Universe.

Early years

Albert Einstein, pictured here with his younger sister, Maja, was born in 1879 in Ulm, Germany. After school, he worked as a clerk in a **patent office** in Switzerland, checking applications for electrical devices. In his spare time, he developed radical theories about **LIGHT AND TIME**. In 1905, he published five scientific papers that would ***change the world***.

Time warp

In his theory of **SPECIAL RELATIVITY**, Einstein showed the Universe is a pretty weird place. He suggested that **space and time are linked** and that they are flexible and can change, depending on who is looking at them. He explained that ***the faster you travel, the slower time passes for you***, and that light has a speed limit of 300,000 km (186,000 miles) per second.

He paved the way for...

The first NUCLEAR BOMB *went off in a massive explosion in 1945. It proved Einstein's* $E=mc^2$ *equation, and released the energy locked in atoms.*

Einstein developed a theory of LASERS. *These are used to read CDs, DVDs, and* BARCODES*... and are often seen in science fiction films.*

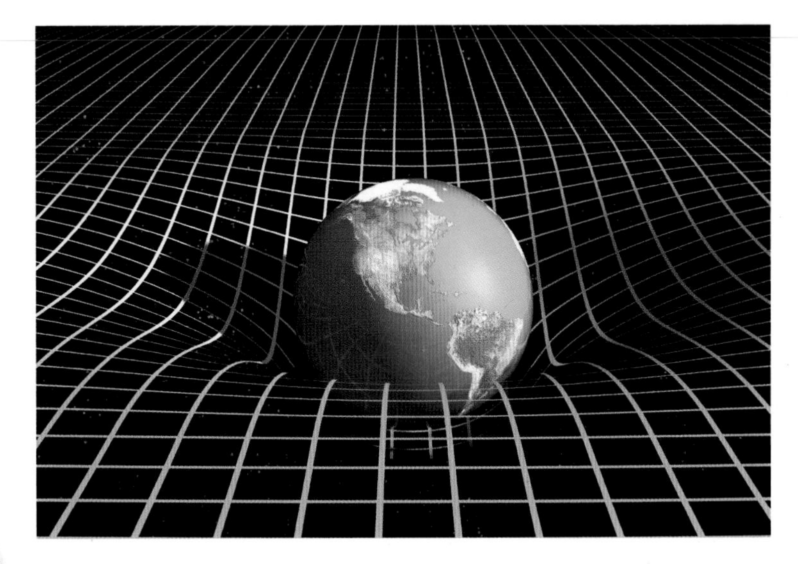

Gravity and the Universe

Isaac Newton believed that gravity is the force of a big object attracting a smaller object. Einstein's theory of **GENERAL RELATIVITY** says that space and time are part of the same thing, which is called "**space–time**", and large objects – such as planets – cause this space-time to ***bend***. Imagine a bowling ball placed on a sheet so that it causes the sheet to bend. Smaller objects wouldn't bend the sheet as much as the heavy ball, so they roll into the dent made by the bigger object. This is gravity.

By the way...
when I was a child, my parents worried that I might be stupid, as I hardly ever spoke and I tried out my sentences by whispering them first.

Inspirational scientist
Einstein's ideas changed physics and astronomy forever. His theories paved the way for decades of discovery, from the smallest known particles, to the largest questions about how the Universe works. Einstein is an icon of creativity and genius.

Did you know?
When Einstein died in 1955, scientists wanted know what made him so clever. So, they took out his brain for testing and discovered that the part responsible for mathematical thought was unusually large in his brain.

Knowledge of relativity means the clocks on **GPS** *(Global Positioning System) satellites – used for guiding car* **SAT NAVS** *– are set to be slow, so they match clocks on the receivers.*

Einstein was suspicious of **Niels Bohr** *(1885–1962) and his quantum mechanics theory, which is essential in making* **MICROCHIPS** *work.*

Marie Curie

The woman who figured out RADIOACTIVITY, was the first woman to win a Nobel Prize, and was also the first person to win two

All about me

- **BORN:** 1867
- **DIED:** 1934
- **NATIONALITY:** Polish
- **FACTOID:** My oldest daughter, Irene, also won the Nobel Prize in Chemistry.
- **IN A NUTSHELL:** Born in Warsaw, Poland, I studied physics and mathematics in Paris, France. There I met Pierre Curie, who became my husband.

By the way... unaware of the dangers, I died of aplastic anaemia (a blood disorder) due to radiation exposure from my own research.

Radioactivity

The Curies worked together to investigate **radioactivity**. Marie proved that the atoms of radioactive elements fire off **HIGH-ENERGY** particles – which we call radiation. This proved that atoms were more than just solid balls. They also discovered two new radioactive elements, called ***polonium*** and ***radium***, and later realized that radiation could be used to treat diseases such as cancer.

The X-factor

Knowing that radioactive elements emit X-rays, Marie improved the ***X-ray machines*** used in hospitals. She created a new machine that was small enough to fit into ambulances and, during the **FIRST WORLD WAR**, her mobile X-ray units were used to diagnose soldiers who were too badly wounded to travel to a hospital.

During the war, Curie herself drove X-ray equipped ambulances to the front lines.

By the way...
during the First World War, I worked on ways of detecting submarines using sound waves.

Ernest Rutherford

The man who discovered the structure of the ATOM, split it apart, and won a Nobel Prize in Chemistry

All about me

- **BORN:** 1871
- **DIED:** 1937
- **NATIONALITY:** New Zealander
- **FACTOID:** I am sometimes called "the father of nuclear physics".
- **IN A NUTSHELL:** Born in New Zealand, I became a professor of physics at McGill University in Canada and investigated the new discovery of radioactivity.

Particle puzzle

After Marie Curie proved that **atoms** weren't just solid balls, Rutherford figured out that most of an atom's mass is at its centre, or **NUCLEUS**, and the rest of the atom is actually made up mostly of empty space. He also realized that the nucleus is made up of smaller particles, called ***protons*** and ***neutrons***, surrounded by a cloud of tiny particles called ***electrons***.

Hydrogen is the only element without any neutrons

Splitting the atom

Rutherford discovered that an atom's nucleus could be **smashed apart** if it is struck by another high-energy particle (like snooker balls smashing together). Using a radioactive source to fire particles at an atom, he found that impact knocked the protons out of the nucleus and ***split*** the atom. Rutherford had created a new science – **NUCLEAR PHYSICS.**

Watson and Crick

The guys who UNCOVERED the secret of life

A chromosome is a package of genetic information made up of a very long strand of DNA.

Watson and Crick were the first to uncover the double helix structure of DNA and unravel what makes us tick.

The dynamic duo

Francis Crick was born in 1916 near Northampton, England. He studied physics, but changed to biology and got a job at ***Cambridge University***. James Watson was born in 1928 in Chicago, USA. He wanted to study ornithology (the study of birds), but changed his mind and took **genetics**. He moved to Cambridge University in 1951, where he met Crick. Watson and Crick worked together on studying the **STRUCTURE OF DNA.**

By the way...
until we came along, scientists knew DNA carried genes from one generation to the next, but they didn't know how – or what DNA looked like.

Did you know?
After they made their discovery, Crick walked into the Eagle pub in Cambridge and announced, "We have found the secret of life".

They couldn't have done it without...

GREGOR MENDEL *(1822–1884) started the* **SCIENCE OF GENETICS**. *He studied peas and discovered they passed on certain traits to their offspring.*

FRIEDRICH MIESCHER *(1844–1895) discovered that cells contain* **NUCLEIC ACIDS**, *which paved the way for the discovery of DNA, a nucleic acid.*

Credit where credit's due

At the same time as Watson and Crick, two scientists at King's College, London, **ROSALIND FRANKLIN** and Maurice Wilkins, were also studying DNA – using X-rays. Wilkins showed Watson a copy of Franklin's work without her permission. They used Franklin's findings in their research, but ***didn't give her the credit she deserved***. Watson, Crick, and Wilkins all shared the **Nobel Prize for Medicine** in 1962, but Franklin received no acknowledgement for her contribution.

DNA can copy itself by unzipping the helix and the nucleotides attract new partners, building two identical helices.

Cracking the code of life

Deoxyribonucleic acid (DNA) is the set of chemical instructions that ***lives in the cells of every creature on Earth***. DNA tells a cell how to behave and grow. Watson and Crick discovered that DNA has two strands that are twisted together like a spiral ladder, called the **DOUBLE HELIX**. Between the strands are special molecules called nucleotides (which had been discovered already). There are **four different nucleotides** (Adenine, Thymine, Cytosine, and Guanine), and the order they are in determines the DNA's instructions.

Science from within

The discovery of DNA's structure opened up whole new branches of science. We can create genetically modified (GM) crops by fiddling with their DNA. Scientists have even mapped the genetic code of humans, which could lead to new cures for diseases, and even prevent them happening.

They paved the way for...

The police can IDENTIFY A CRIMINAL *from the DNA he or she leaves behind. This is called* FORENSIC (OR GENETIC) FINGERPRINTING.

Scientists can CLONE *an animal by making a copy of its DNA. The first mammal ever cloned was* DOLLY THE SHEEP, *in 1996.*

Mary Anning

The FOSSIL hunter who found dinosaur bones beneath her feet, and changed our view of evolution

All about me

- **BORN:** 1799
- **DIED:** 1847
- **NATIONALITY:** English
- **FACTOID:** As a baby, I survived being struck by lightning.
- **IN A NUTSHELL:** I was born in Lyme Regis, Dorset, UK, an area that is very famous for its fossils.

Fearsome fossils

Mary spent most of her time searching Lyme Regis beach for **FOSSILS** with her brother, Joseph. When she was 12, Joseph found the first fossil ***ichthyosaur*** (above) and Mary excavated it. Mary discovered the first almost complete ***plesiosaur*** and the first ***pterosaur*** outside of Germany. She even found a fish that was the **missing link** between sharks and rays.

By the way... I used to search the beach during fierce storms to find any fossils that the crashing waves might have exposed.

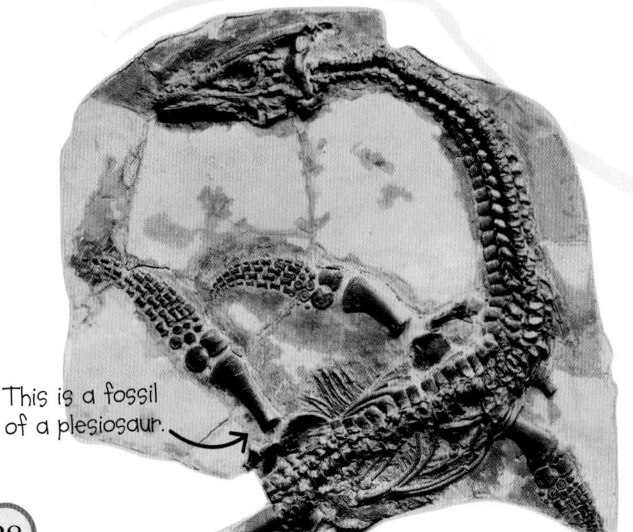

Evolution revolution

Mary made her **discoveries** at a time when most people believed the biblical creation story, stating that God created everything as it is today. The spectacular creatures that Mary uncovered, like the plesiosaur, were so ***unlike anything still alive today*** that they forced scientists to accept that the natural world changed gradually over time. Her work helped to guide science towards the **THEORY OF EVOLUTION.**

All about me

- **BORN:** 1913
- **DIED:** 1996
- **NATIONALITY:** English
- **FACTOID:** I developed a new system for classifying ancient stone tools.
- **IN A NUTSHELL:** Born in London, UK, I spent most of my life searching for human fossils and artefacts in Africa.

Hunting hominins

Mary had an amazing ability to find fossil ***hominins*** (ancient relatives of today's humans). In 1959, in the Olduvai Gorge, Tanzania, she found the **SKULL** of a human ancestor she nicknamed the "Nutcracker Man", as he had huge jaws and teeth. Later, she found the skull and hand of a species she called "**handy-man**", which was very closely related to modern humans.

"Nutcracker Man" lived in Africa around 1.75 million years ago.

By the way... my obsession with early humans began when my dad took me to see cave paintings in France when I was 12.

A step ahead

Mary's most exciting discovery, in 1978, was a set of ancient **FOOTPRINTS** in Laetoli, Tanzania. They showed that humans began walking upright much ***earlier*** than scientists had thought. Mary is seen as one of the world's best **archaeologists**, scientists who specialize in unearthing the past. Her discoveries revealed a lot about where humans first came from.

The Laetoli fossilized footprints are more than 3.75 million years old.

Mary Leakey

The woman who found the SKELETONS in mankind's closet, and showed us where humans came from

Inspirational

Inventors

Without these bright sparks, your daily life would be very different. You wouldn't be writing on paper, or travelling by car. In fact, you wouldn't be reading this book. Imagine life without phones, jeans, planes, TV, Facebook, and fast food. Sure, life would go on, but these ingenious inventors have made the world a much more high-tech, versatile, and exciting place to be.

All about me

- **BORN:** 50
- **DIED:** 121
- **NATIONALITY:** Chinese
- **FACTOID:** I was an official in the court of Emperor He of Han.
- **IN A NUTSHELL:** Born in Guiyang (modern-day Leiyang), China, I was made an official in charge of manufacturing instruments and weapons.

Cai Lun

The man who mashed up tree bark, created PAPER, and changed the world of writing

A little heavy reading

Before the invention of paper, reading was a heavyweight pastime. Civilizations, such as the Mesopotamians, wrote on heavy **clay tablets**. In China, books were made of ***bamboo***, which wasn't very flexible, or from very expensive silk. In the West, at that time, people were still making notes on wax tablets and using papyrus or **ANIMAL SKINS** to write on.

Paper is still made in much the same way today.

By the way... the Europeans wrote on parchment, which was made from the skins of baby animals.

Paper didn't get to Europe until the 12th century

A barking idea

In 105, Cai invented paper. He took the soft inner bark of a **mulberry tree**, added bamboo fibres, and mixed in some water. He **GAVE THE MIXTURE A GOOD POUNDING**, poured it out over some woven cloth, and let the water drain away. When it was dry, only the fibres were left behind... and Cai had a sheet of paper! The invention of paper allowed ***ideas and knowledge to be spread much faster***.

Paper was made in huge sheets and then cut down to size.

造紙 蔡倫

ıll about me

BORN: 1398
DIED: 1468
NATIONALITY: German
FACTOID: I was a printer nd publisher.
IN A NUTSHELL: Born in Mainz, ;ermany, I invented the ›rinting press – one of ıe most important ıventions of the ıodern era.

Johann Gutenberg

The man who helped put a BOOK in everyone's hands, and opened up reading to the masses

Secret experiments

Gutenberg ***enjoyed reading*** and thought it was a pity that only rich people could afford to buy books. In a **secret workshop** he experimented with individual, movable letters, and new oil-based inks. For his printing press, he adapted the presses that were for winemaking at the time. In 1454, he was successful, and he printed his landmark book, the **GUTENBERG BIBLE**.

ıutenberg's first ible cost about hree years' wages ıt the time... they ıot cheaper.

Gutenberg experimented with wooden type, but ended up using metal letters because they didn't smudge.

‹eading evolution

ıews of Gutenberg's nnovation **soon ›pread around ›urope** and, before ıe died, presses like ıis were at work in all ›urope's great cities. The ›rinting press allowed ideas ınd information to spread ike never before, so that ›veryone, rich or poor, ›ould **ENJOY READING**.

By the way... my secretive work left some of my neighbours believing I was a wizard who had secret meetings with the devil!

James Watt

The inventor whose engine STEAMED ahead

By the way... the watt, a unit of measurement of electrical and mechanical power, is named in my honour.

James Watt didn't invent the steam engine, but his changes made it cheaper to run. His engines powered the Industrial Revolution and changed the world forever.

Young engineer

James Watt was born in Greenock, Scotland, in 1736. The son of a wealthy ship-builder, Watt started off building and repairing mathematical instruments at the University of Glasgow, but quickly took an interest in steam engines.

Hot talent

The first commercially successful **steam engine** was built in 1712 by the English inventor Thomas Newcomen as a way to pump water. Watt noticed that these engines wasted a lot of fuel because the cylinder had to be repeatedly heated and cooled, which required **A LOT OF ENERGY**. In 1769, Watt designed a new engine where the cylinder ***stayed hot*** – it was far more efficient, using just a quarter of the fuel of the old design.

He paved the way for...

Watt's engine was improved by English engineer **RICHARD TREVITHICK** *(1771–1833) who used it to build the first* **STEAM TRAIN** *in 1804.*

In 1829, English inventor **GEORGE STEPHENSON** *(1741–1848) built the most advanced train of its day, the* **ROCKET**, *and the first public train line.*

Steaming ahead

Up until Watt made his changes, the steam engine was used mainly to **pump water** from mines. Knowing that his new engine could be used for so much more, Watt took on a business partner called Matthew Boulton (1728–1829) to help market it. With Boulton's help, **IT WAS A GREAT SUCCESS**, and, by 1783, it had almost completely replaced the old Newcomen model.

Watt on Earth

Watt's engine designs were the driving force behind decades of social and economic change that are still being felt today. However, apart from the steam engine, Watt also invented the process of manufacturing chlorine on a large scale, for use in bleaching.

Watt's engine began the shift of people's reliance on animal labour to machinery.

Power to the people

Soon steam engines were being used to power **all sorts of machinery**. Watt's engines were used to pump drinking water, drive water wheels, turn mills, and drain docks. His engine provided the power that drove the **INDUSTRIAL REVOLUTION**, when people began to rely on machinery. This led to a period of rapid urban growth, and soon many people ***abandoned the countryside*** and moved into cities.

Watt came up with the term "horsepower" to explain how much work his steam engines could do.

In 1884, English engineer **CHARLES PARSONS** *(1854–1931) developed the first steam turbine. Ten years later, the first steam turbine-powered ship, the* **TURBINIA** *was built.*

Steam turbines are at the heart of every modern-day **POWER PLANT**. *The turbines are used to convert the steam power into electricity.*

Alessandro Volta

The man who gave the world its first BATTERY and unlocked the secrets of electricity

By the way... my name is on every battery. The amount of electrical potential a battery has is measured in "volts" (named after me).

All about me

■ **BORN:** 1745
■ **DIED:** 1827
■ **NATIONALITY:** Italian
■ **FACTOID:** I discovered methane gas.
■ **IN A NUTSHELL:** I was born in Como, Italy. I was a professor of experimental physics and I spent most of my life studying electricity.

Getting a leg up

In 1786, an Italian anatomist, Luigi Galvani, discovered he could make a frog's leg twitch when he **pressed steel rods against it**. Volta realized that the wet leg caused an **ELECTRIC CURRENT** to run between the steel rods and the tin plate beneath the frog. The key to this was the ***two different metals***.

The voltaic pile was the forerunner of modern batteries.

When Volta demonstrated his device to Napoleon, he made Volta a count.

Volta's battery

Volta tried to recreate the effect in his own way. In 1800, he used **discs of copper and zinc** for the different metals and, to replace the frog's leg, he used cardboard soaked in salt water. When he stacked them up in layers, ***electricity flowed through the pile***. Volta called the device a "voltaic pile". He had just **INVENTED THE BATTERY**.

Michael Faraday

The man who invented the electric MOTOR and the electric generator

.ll about me

BORN: 1791
DIED: 1867
NATIONALITY: English
FACTOID: My face has een on the £20 note.
IN A NUTSHELL: I was orn near London, England. ıy father was a blacksmith, nd I had very little ɔrmal education.

By the way...
I discovered that a metal "Faraday" cage can protect whatever is inside from a huge electric current, by conducting it safely around the cage.

ʌ notion of motion

ı 1821, Faraday showed that when you ow electricity through a coil of wire, it reates a ***magnetic field***. He realized ıat this electromagnetic energy could be sed to produce **motion,** and invented the **LECTRIC MOTOR**, which is still used in ountless ways today.

When a copper disc is spun past the poles of the magnet, it produces electricity.

Faraday designed the first transformer.

ʌll in a spin

araday continued to xperiment with magnetism, nd, in 1831, he realized that ' he ***reversed his process*** he ould produce an electrical urrent. By spinning a copper isc between the poles of a ıagnet, he could **generate a teady flow of electricity** through wire. Faraday had invented the first **ɔYNAMO** (pictured above), which would ventually become the electric generator.

These are now used to turn high voltages into low ones that are safe enough to use in our homes.

Everyday inventions

INVENTING stuff we can't live without

Every so often, someone comes along and invents something that makes us wonder how we ever did without it. Here are the people behind some of those "must have" inventions.

Charles Goodyear

(1800–1860)

If your car's tyres were made of natural rubber, they would **melt in the summer and freeze in the winter**... pretty useless. Fortunately, this American inventor worked out how to **VULCANIZE** (harden) rubber by ***heating*** it and mixing it with chemicals.

Levi Strauss

(1829–1902)

Can you imagine Elvis wearing corduroy? An American tailor named Jacob Davis started **putting metal rivets on work trousers** to give them ***extra strength***. His business partner, a German named Levi Strauss, patented, produced, and promoted the new "**JEANS**".

Jeans became a rock and roll fashion ico

George Eastman
(1854–1932)

Today you're more likely to use your phone to take a photograph, but before the iPhone, there was Kodak. Eastman was an American inventor who brought ***roll film*** to market, which replaced expensive **photographic plates**. He also invented a small, cheap camera, called the **KODAK** in 1888.

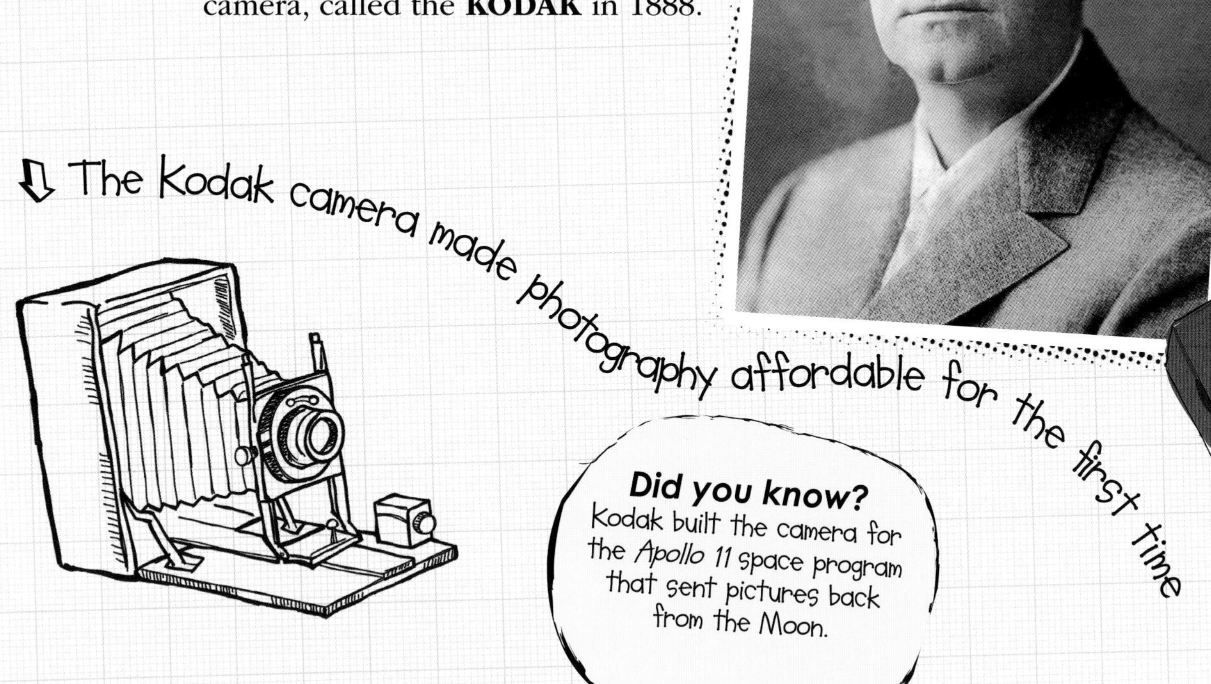

Wallace Carothers
(1896–1937)

This American chemist has been helping women cover their legs for more than 70 years. He created **NYLON**, the first **synthetic polymer** (a bit like plastic), which, when pulled out into threads, can be used to make anything from ***guitar strings to stockings***.

The first nylon stockings were worn only by movie stars

Alexander Graham Bell

The man whose invention got the world TALKING, and made it seem a little bit smaller

All about me

- **BORN:** 1847
- **DIED:** 1922
- **NATIONALITY:** Scottish
- **FACTOID:** I also invented the first metal detector.
- **IN A NUTSHELL:** I was born in Edinburgh, Scotland, but lived and worked in both the US and Canada.

The first words spoken by telephone were: "Mr Watson, come here, I want to see you".

The electrical speech machine

Long-distance messages were once sent by telegraph, which sent electronic code through cables. Bell suspected that he could use the telegraph wires to ***transmit a human voice***. In 1875, with the help of American Thomas Watson (1854–1934), he created the first **electrical speech machine** or, as it is now known, the **TELEPHONE**. By 1878, Bell had set up the world's first telephone exchange in Connecticut, USA.

By the way... the American inventor Elisha Gray (1835–1901) also invented a version of the telephone, but I beat him to the patent and got all the credit.

Work with the deaf

It was Bell's work with the deaf that eventually led him to invent the telephone and the microphone. ***Bell's mother was deaf***, and his father had developed a **VISIBLE SPEECH SYSTEM** to help deaf children learn to speak. In 1872, Bell opened the School of Vocal Physiology and Mechanics of Speech (pictured left) in Boston to help train teachers to **help deaf children** use his father's system.

Thomas Edison

A prolific inventor whose ideas helped to make the world a much BRIGHTER place for everybody

All about me

- **BORN:** 1847
- **DIED:** 1931
- **NATIONALITY:** American
- **FACTOID:** I patented almost 1,100 inventions.
- **IN A NUTSHELL:** I was born in Ohio, USA. By the time I was 12, I was almost completely deaf. I didn't really mind though – it helped me to concentrate!

By the way... I also held patents for the phonograph (a music player) and a kinetograph (motion picture recorder).

A thin wire (filament) glows when electricity is passed through it.

Let there be light

The **FILAMENTS** of early light bulbs were too bright and burned out after just a few hours. Edison did **4,700 experiments** to find a better material and, in 1879, he tried using carbon and created a light bulb that lasted 1,500 hours, ***making the bulb practical for the first time ever***.

Electric revolution

To make his invention useful, people needed an **ELECTRICITY SUPPLY**. So Edison invented a way to produce electricity and distribute it through wires into homes and businesses. In 1882, he built the first public power station, the ***Edison Electric Light Station*** in London, UK, and eight months later, he built America's first power station in New York, USA. By the 1890s, **hundreds of towns** throughout the world had Edison power stations, and soon electricity became part of everyday life.

Alfred Nobel

The man who put the BANG into peace

In life Nobel invented new ways to blow things up, but in death his name promotes peace and learning.

Young chemist

Alfred Nobel was born in 1833 in Stockholm, Sweden. His **father was an engineer and inventor**. In 1842, his family moved to Russia where his father started an engineering firm that built ***equipment for the army of the Tsar*** (Russia's king). When he was 17, Nobel was sent abroad to study **CHEMICAL ENGINEERING.**

Making a bang

Nobel was fascinated by **EXPLOSIVES** and wanted to make them safer – in particular nitroglycerine, which was very **unstable and dangerous** (it could explode if you dropped it). He mixed it with a type of silica, which made it much more stable and safer to work with. Nobel called the new explosive ***"dynamite"*** and it made him very rich.

He couldn't have done it without...

RAGNAR SOHLMAN *(1870–1948) spent five years turning Nobel's slightly vague will into the Nobel Prize we know today.*

BERTHA VON SUTTNER *(1843–1914) was a* PEACE CAMPAIGNER *who influenced Nobel to include a* PRIZE FOR PEACE *in his will.*

By the way...
I thought that dynamite would end war. I believed that when people saw its destructive power, they would be afraid to attack each other.

The environmentalist Wangari Maathi was the first African woman to receive the Nobel Prize.

The road to peace

In 1888, Nobel got a shock when he saw his **obituary in a newspaper.** It called him the "merchant of death". In fact, his brother, Ludvig, had died, but they had published Alfred's obituary by mistake. Alfred didn't want to be remembered like this, so, when he really did die, he ***left most of his fortune*** to set up a prize that would celebrate great achievements in peace and learning. This became known as the **NOBEL PRIZE.**

Dynamite has been used in blast mining and to build canals, railways, and roads.

A Nobel pursuit

The first Nobel Prizes in Physics, Chemistry, Physiology (or Medicine), Literature, and Peace were awarded in 1901. Since then, the prize has become the greatest award for achievement in the world. It contributes to the progress of science and culture, and the promotion of peace... all because a newspaper made a mistake.

Alfred's little brother was killed in an explosion when an experiment went wrong

Many big engineering projects, like the **Hoover Dam** *in the United States (constructed between 1931 and 1936) were only possible because of the* **BLASTING POWER** *of dynamite.*

He paved the way for...

Food made easy

Not so long ago, if you wanted food to last, you grew turnips. For fast food, you ate the turnip raw. These men changed all that.

The men who made FOOD more convenient

Did you know?
The first tin cans were so thick they had to be hammered open. The can opener wasn't invented for another 50 years.

Peter Durand
(1766–1822)

The Napoleonic wars were raging in Europe and the army needed a way of **safely feeding its soldiers**. The British merchant Peter Durand heard that the French were ***preserving food*** in glass bottles by heating the food so it became sterilized. As bottles break easily, Durand came up with the idea of using **TIN CANS** instead of fragile bottles.

Durand invented the first tin can in 1810 ⇨

Clarence Birdseye
(1886–1956)

The American inventor Clarence Birdseye was working in the Arctic when he noticed that fish caught by the locals were almost **instantly frozen** by the icy winds. As it had frozen so quickly, the fish still ***tasted great***, so, when he got home to New York, USA, he copied the **FLASH-FREEZING** process.

⇩ Birdseye invented his flash-freezing process in 1924

Percy Spencer
(1894–1970)

Percy Spencer was an American engineer who built machines that were used to generate microwaves. One day he was **standing too close** to one of his machines when he noticed the chocolate bar in his pocket had ***melted***. He experimented with popcorn and realized **MICROWAVES** could be used for cooking.

Ray Kroc
(1902–1984)

From a **high school drop out** to a successful American businessman, Ray Kroc was the man who thought that fast food was too slow. He came up with the idea that, if he used ***Henry Ford's production line techniques***, food could be made much faster. In 1955, he used his idea in a small restaurant called **McDONALD'S**.

Guglielmo Marconi

The inventor of the first RADIO SYSTEM who received the Nobel Prize in Physics

All about me

- **BORN:** 1874
- **DIED:** 1937
- **NATIONALITY:** Italian
- **FACTOID:** I was an engineer and physicist.
- **IN A NUTSHELL:** Born in Bologna, Italy, I was a bad student, but was fascinated with science and electricity.

The radio star

As a young man, Marconi read about Heinrich Hertz's **discovery of radio waves**. He wondered if you could use radio waves to transmit information without using wires. He started experimenting, and could soon operate a bell wirelessly. His ***first long-distance transmission*** was in 1896, when he sent a message to a receiver 1.6 km (1 mile) away. In 1897, he started the **MARCONI COMPANY**.

When the radio stations started transmitting sound, Marconi's company started building radio sets.

By the way... when I died at age 63, radio stations all over the world observed a two-minute silence as a tribute.

Early radio systems sent messages using a series of dots and dashes called Morse code.

Titanic achievement

Seeing its potential, the British and Indian navies adopted Marconi's ***wireless telegraph system***, and by 1901, he was able to send messages across the Atlantic. Marconi's radio proved its worth in 1912 onboard the **TITANIC**. As the ship sank, its radio operators signalled for help. Two ships heard the distress call and came to its aid, **saving 700 lives**.

John Logie Baird

The man who invented the first TELEVISION, and gave the world something to watch

All about me

- **BORN:** 1888
- **DIED:** 1946
- **NATIONALITY:** Scottish
- **FACTOID:** I was an engineer and inventor.
- **IN A NUTSHELL:** As a child, I built a telephone exchange in my bedroom so I could talk with my friends.

By the way... when I was in my twenties, I tried to make diamonds by heating graphite, but only managed to short out Glasgow's electricity supply.

Baird started selling TVs in 1930, but the spinning disc made them very noisy.

The TV star

Scientists had been **trying to build a television for decades**. Baird's first attempt was quite crude, and was made of odds and ends, but, by 1924, he had managed to ***transmit a flickering image*** a short distance. In 1926, he demonstrated the **WORLD'S FIRST TELEVISION** to 50 scientists in London.

The mechanical televison

Baird's television wasn't the electronic device we know today, but was more like a **CLOCKWORK MACHINE**. It used a **spinning cardboard disc**, which had a series of square holes stamped into it. As the disc span, each hole scanned a different part of the image. His TV produced a ***tiny, flickering 30-line picture***, where modern TVs produce more than 1,000 lines... not exactly high definition.

The Wright brothers

The fathers of powered FLIGHT

By the way... we tossed a coin to see who would fly first. Wilbur won, but the engine stalled, so it was Orville's attempt that made it into the history books.

These pioneers made the first ever sustained, powered flight. Before them, flight was a useless novelty – they turned it into the transportation of the future.

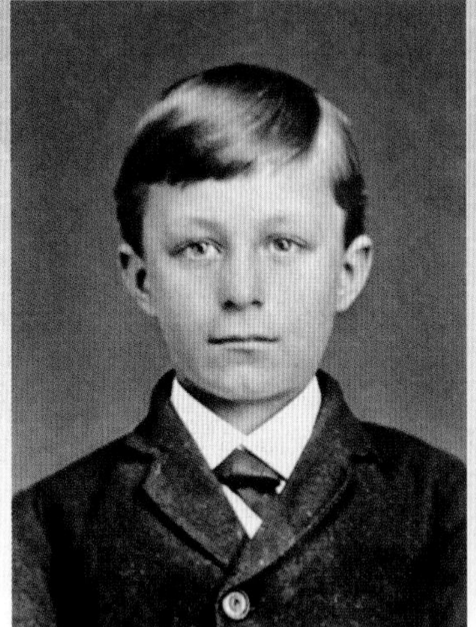

Wilbur Wright

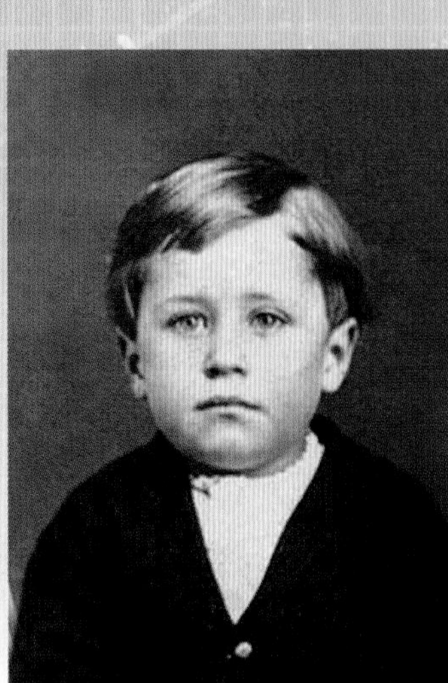

Orville Wright

Young tinkers

Wilbur Wright was born in 1867 in Indiana, USA, and his brother, Orville, was born four years later. From an early age the boys were ***obsessed*** with all things **MECHANICAL** and with the idea of flight. By 1895, they started building their own bicycles, but it wasn't long before they started to dream about building their own **flying machines**.

Things look up

Wilbur wrote to the Smithsonian Institute – a famous museum in Washington DC, USA – and asked for all the information they had on aeronautics (the science of flight). The brothers studied **BIRDS** and used what they had learned to build their own **gliders**. They built a wind tunnel to test all their designs, but soon realized that, if their flying machine were to travel any distance, it would need something to ***propel*** it.

They couldn't have done it without...

Wilbur was inspired to build an AIRCRAFT *when he read about German glider pilot* OTTO LILIENTHAL *(1848–1896), an early pioneer of aviation.*

Orville takes to the air in the Wright Flyer.

Flying high

The brothers started work on building their own **ENGINE** and created a completely new propeller design with blades based on the shape of a wing. By 1903, their powered glider was ready for a test flight and, on 17 December, the ***Wright Flyer*** took to the air with Orville at the helm. Their first attempt lasted just 12 seconds and they travelled only 36.5 m (120 ft), but they had achieved their **childhood dream**.

Up, up, and away!

The sky's (not) the limit

At the time the Wright brothers made their famous flight, it could take up to three weeks to sail across the Atlantic. Today, the same distance is covered in just a few hours by aeroplane. The brother's invention brought the world closer together and was the first step in mankind's journey to the Moon and beyond.

They paved the way for...

Giant passenger aircraft were made possible by the invention of the **JET ENGINE** *by English engineer* **FRANK WHITTLE** *(1907–1996).*

Just 58 years after Orville's first flight, a Russian called **YURI GAGARIN** *(1934–1968) became the first human to fly into* **SPACE**.

Henry Ford

The man who DROVE the world to change

Henry Ford pioneered the use of assembly lines and transformed the car from a luxury item for the rich into a method of transport everyone could afford.

First gear

Henry Ford was born in Dearborn, Michigan, USA, in 1863. He grew up on the family farm and loved tinkering and ***experimenting*** with machinery. After he built his first horseless carriage in 1896, he met the inventor **THOMAS EDISON**, who encouraged Ford to build more.

A car for the masses

Ford wanted to build a car that everyone could afford and, in 1908, his Ford Motor Company created the **MODEL T**. Ford's assembly lines meant that he could produce the Model T **faster and cheaper** than any other car manufacturer. While cars at the time cost almost $3,000, Ford sold the Model T for ***just $825***.

At its height, a new Model T was built every 24 seconds!

Did you know?
Ford improved working conditions in his factories by increasing pay and reducing working hours.

He couldn't have done it without...

In 1804, the American inventor **Oliver Evans** *(1755–1819) invented a steam-powered land vehicle called the* **Oruktor Amphibolis**.

In 1885, the German engineer **Karl Benz** *(1844–1929) built the* **first automobile** *powered by an internal combustion engine.*

By the way...
I got the idea for using conveyor belts on my assembly line when I saw them being used in a pig slaughter house.

Putting it all together

Ford thought that the old method of building a car was too ***inefficient***. Instead of using a few people to assemble an entire car, he decided that each part of the assembly would be done by one person and then passed down a **conveyor belt** to the next person until, at the end of the line, they had built a complete a car. Ford's technique **CUT THE TIME** it took to build a chassis from 12 hours to just an hour and a half.

The Model T was originally available in green, red, blue, and grey, but after 1913 they were made only in black.

The Model T came in lots of different shapes: Touring, Runabout, Coupé, Town, Tourster, Torpedo, Sedan, and Couplet.

The road ahead

Ford's improved assembly line revolutionized industry and his techniques are still used today – but with more robots! His Model T, which sold more than 15 million, started the "age of the motorcar". Suddenly people all over the world could travel wherever they wanted.

Another German, **GOTTLIEB DAIMLER** *(1834–1900), invented the world's first* **HIGH-SPEED PETROL ENGINE** *and the very first four-wheeled automobile.*

In 1901, the American inventor **RANDSOM E OLDS** *(1864–1950) was the first person to use an* **ASSEMBLY LINE** *to build his cars.*

Steve Jobs & Steve Wozniak

The guys who gave us HOME COMPUTERS

Once upon a time, personal computers had to be put together from a kit and could be used only by highly skilled super-geeks. Apple changed all this.

The two Steves

Both Californians, Steve Wozniak was born in 1950 in Sunnyvale, USA, and loved tinkering with electronics. Steve Jobs was born in San Francisco, USA, in 1955 and grew up in the area that would become **Silicon Valley.** The pair first met when Jobs got a summer job at Hewlett Packard where Wozniak was also working. In 1976, they both quit their jobs to create "**APPLE**". Their goal was to create ***a cheap computer that was easy to use.***

The iPad is a touch-screen computer that lets you browse the Internet, watch movies, play games, and read e-books.

By the way... I sold my Volkswagen van and Woz sold his prized scientific calculator so that we had enough money to build the Apple I.

Binary code is a sort of compu language that uses the digits 0 and 1 to represent data. Th letter "i" in binary is 01101001.

They couldn't have done it without...

The first "computer" was built by **Charles Babbage** *(1791–1871) in the 1820s. His "Difference Engine" was a machine that performed* **MATHEMATICAL CALCULATIONS**.

Alan Turing *(1912–1954) designed the* **FIRST MODERN COMPUTER** *to use binary code and magnetic tape to store data in 1936.*

Before Apple I, computers were just circuit boards and switches.

The "i" in iMac stands for "Internet" because it was Internet-ready.

The home computer is born

Wozniak dismantled a calculator and realized that the **MICROCHIP** was the key to building a cheap computer. Just a few months after leaving their jobs, they had built their first computer – the **Apple I**. Apple released the "Macintosh" in 1984, which was the first computer to have a ***graphical user interface (GUI)***, which allowed users to interact with icons on the screen.

By the way... I was the brains and engineering talent behind Apple's early products, but I left in 1981 after suffering short-term memory loss in a plane crash.

"i" will take over the world

By the 1990s, PCs ruled the computing world and Apple was in trouble. They needed to do something **REVOLUTIONARY** again. So, in 1998, they released the iMac, which had a built-in monitor. In 2001 came the iPod, the ***bestselling portable music player***. The iPhone, launched in 2007, became the **biggest selling mobile phone in history** and, in 2010, they unveiled their tablet computer, the iPad.

Planet Apple

Early Apple computers set the standard for the home computer industry. More recently, Apple has created revolutionary lifestyle devices that have changed the way we communicate.

The microchip is used in almost every electronic device.

The TRANSISTOR*, released in the 1950s, revolutionized modern electronics and made* CHEAP GADGETS *possible. It is used to amplify and switch electronic signals.*

ROBERT NOYCE *(1927–1990) and* JACK KILBY *(1923–2005) invented the* INTEGRATED CIRCUIT *(microchip) in 1959, which made modern computing possible.*

Tim Berners-Lee

The computer geek who used the WORLD WIDE WEB to connect the world

All about me

- **BORN:** 1955
- **NATIONALITY:** English
- **FACTOID:** I am a computer scientist.
- **ANOTHER FACTOID:** I was caught hacking when I was at Oxford University.
- **IN A NUTSHELL:** I worked as a software engineer for the European Organization for Nuclear Research (CERN) in Geneva, Switzerland.

By the way... my invention could have made me very rich, but I wanted the Internet to be free for everyone.

```
                                                              CERN Welcom
      CERN

   The European Laboratory for Particle Physics, located near  Geneva[1] in
   Switzerland[2] and  France[3].  Also the birthplace of the  World-Wide
   Web[4].

   This is the CERN laboratory main server. The support team provides a set of
   Services[5] to the physics experiments and the lab. For questions and
   suggestions, see WWW Support Contacts[6] at CERN
   ___________________________________________
   About the Laboratory[7] - Hot News[8] -  Activities[9] - About Physics[10] -
    Other Subjects[11] - Search[12]
   ___________________________________________

About the Laboratory

     Help[13] and  General information[14], divisions, groups and
     activities[15] (structure),  Scientific committees[16]

     Directories[17] (phone & email, services & people), Scientific
     Information Service[18] (library, archives or Alice), Preprint[19] Server

1-45, Back, Up, <RETURN> for more, Quit, or Help:
```

Creating the web

In 1991, Tim created the **World Wide Web** so that people would have an easy way to access the information stored on the Internet, the global network of computers and servers. His first **WEBSITE** wasn't very impressive – it was just green and black – but it changed the way we ***access information*** forever.

A webpage is created and the information is uploaded onto a server.

The information is stored on servers and split into small packets of code.

A web browser decodes these packets and displays them in a web browser.

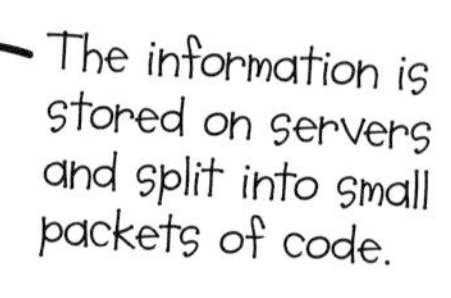

A use for the Internet

The **Internet** was created in 1969, but only used to link computers at different American universities. The World Wide Web – invented by Berners-Lee more than 20 years later – is really a collection of ***hyperlinked documents called websites*** that is made possible by the Internet. Tim also created the world's first **WEB BROWSER**, which is a computer program that allows people to find, view, and interact with these websites.

Mark Zuckerberg

The young fella who created FACEBOOK, got very rich, and turned people into friends

By the way...
I am colour-blind, so I made Facebook mostly blue because I can't tell the difference between red and green.

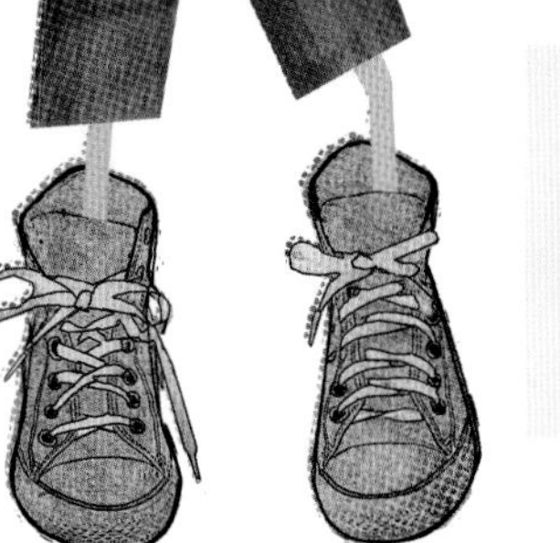

All about me

- **BORN:** 1984
- **NATIONALITY:** American
- **FACTOID:** Facebook's first head office was in my bedroom.
- **ANOTHER FACTOID:** Facebook was originally called "The Facebook".
- **IN A NUTSHELL:** I was born in White Plains, New York, USA, and I was very good at science at school.

Whiz kid

When Mark was 12, he created a messaging program called "**ZUCKNET**", and while he was at high school he designed an online music programme, called "Synapse". Then, at ***Harvard University***, he invented "Facemash", which allowed people to **compare student's faces** and rate how attractive they were.

Face of success

n 2004, Mark created **FACEBOOK**, which llowed users to create their own profiles, upload photos, and ***communicate with their friends***. To start with, the website was just for students at Harvard, but Mark and his friends soon **expanded** to include other universities and then everyone all around the world.

Profile: Build your page so your friends can find out more about you.

Friends: Use the menu to see a list of all of your friends.

Wall: This is where you keep up to date with friends, and post messages and photos.

Events: Tell people about an upcoming birthday party using the events page.

Thoughtful

Thinkers

When this brainy bunch put their thinking caps on, they came up with some new and very influential ideas. Some tried to figure out how the world works, while others decided to do something about suffering and injustice. Whether philosophers, religious leaders, human rights activists, or conservationists, these trailblazers all gave us something to think about.

Confucius

The Chinese PHILOSOPHER who accidentally started a new religion

Confucius taught China's rulers to take better care of their people. His simple yet powerful ideas still influence governments today.

Scraping a living

Confucius was born in 551 BCE near Qufu, China. His once rich **aristocratic family** had fallen on **HARD TIMES**, so Confucius did many things to earn a living, including working as a shepherd and bookkeeper.

In his lessons, Confucius encouraged his students to find knowledge by asking questions.

Path to knowledge

Confucius began teaching when he was about 30 years old. He believed that ***everyone had the right to education*** no matter what their social standing. He opened a **SCHOOL** in his home and even allowed some of his poorer students to live with him. Confucius also worked as a minor official in the state of Lu, but he quickly became **concerned** about what he saw there.

He paved the way for...

The philosopher **MENCIUS** *(390–305 BCE) developed Confucius's teachings, and declared that people had the* **RIGHT TO OVERTHROW AN UNJUST RULER.**

SHI HUANGDI *(259–210 BCE), used Confucius's ideas to unify China and become its first emperor. He also built the* **GREAT WALL OF CHINA.**

禮
Li is the virtue of correct behaviour and propriety.

仁
Ren is the virtue of charity and humanity.

義
Yi is the virtue of honesty and integrity.

孝
Zhi is the virtue of knowledge and learning.

信
Xin is the virtue of faithfulness and loyalty.

By the way... my real name is K'ung Ch'iu, but my followers called me "K'ung Fu-tzu" (Great Master K'ung), which became Confucius in the west.

Leading by example

Confucius realized that government **corruption was everywhere**. Rulers did as they pleased, even testing new weapons on their servants. He developed a new moral code, called the "**FIVE VIRTUES**". He believed that for a society to be happy and prosperous, you need a good government run by good officials. He left his post as an offical and spent 12 years travelling, teaching, and gathering students and disciples. He became a minister in the state of Lu, and used his methods to virtually ***eliminate crime*** and unrest.

During his travels around China, Confucius attracted a following of students and disciples.

The accidental religion

By 136 BCE, Confucius's teachings became the state religion of China, known as Confucianism. For more than 2,000 years all Chinese officials had to pass an exam based on his ideas. Even today, many of the world's governments and religions are still influenced by his philosophies.

The Chinese philosopher and scholar **ZHU XI** *(1130–1200 CE) updated and added to the ideas behind Confucianism, and greatly* **INFLUENCED CHINESE GOVERNMENT**.

Confucius's philosophies were used by America's third president **THOMAS JEFFERSON** *(1743–1826) when he drafted America's* **DECLARATION OF INDEPENDENCE**.

Aristotle

The philosopher who tried to MAKE SENSE of the world

This Greek philosopher was a student of Plato, and the teacher of Alexander the Great. He is also considered to be the father of the modern scientific method.

By the way...
I once said that flies have four legs and, although anyone can see they have six, books repeated my mistake for more than 1,000 years.

Thirst for knowledge

Aristotle was born in Stageira, Greece, in 384 BCE. His father, Nicomachus, was the **personal doctor** to King Amyntas of Macedon. Had his father not died when Aristotle was 10, he would have ***followed his father's trade***, but instead he became interested in the pursuit of **KNOWLEDGE**.

Aristotle wore a simple robe-like garment wrapped about his body called a "himation".

Student and teacher

Aristotle (in blue) joined **Plato's Academy** in Athens when he was 17. Seen in red, Plato (429–347 BCE) – a student of the philosopher Socrates (469–399 BCE) – made his academy the centre of learning in Greece. Aristotle stayed there for 20 years, but when Plato died he left Athens, and, in 342 BCE, he travelled to Macedon to tutor ***Alexander the Great***. He returned to Athens in 335 BCE, and started his own school, the **LYCEUM**.

He paved the way for...

Aristotle's successor at the Lyceum, **THEOPHRASTUS** *(371–287 BCE), pioneered the* **SCIENCE OF BOTANY**, *and influenced scientists for more than 2,000 years.*

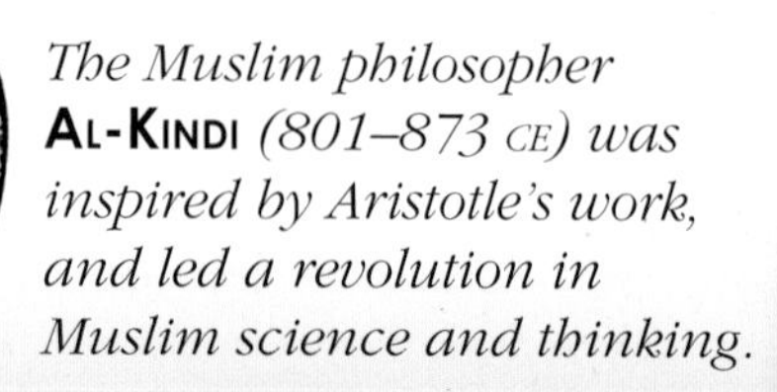

The Muslim philosopher **AL-KINDI** *(801–873 CE) was inspired by Aristotle's work, and led a revolution in Muslim science and thinking.*

Searching for order

Aristotle used **Socrates's method of logic** to try and figure out how the world worked. He tried to ***classify plants and animals*** in a way that would make sense. For example, he grouped animals that seemed similar into two groups: those with red blood and those without red blood. He then divided those groups into **SPECIES**.

Aristotle was the first person to realize that whales and dolphins were not fish.

Aristotle stuttered when he spoke

Great thinker

Aristotle wrote about **DIFFERENT SUBJECTS**, from poetry and theatre, to ethics and politics. He used his system of logic to organize different **types of governments**, classifying monarchies, tyrannies, democracies, and republics, which we still use today. However, he also ***made mistakes***. He thought that the Universe is a sphere with Earth in its centre, and it wasn't until Copernicus (1473–1543) and Galileo (1564–1642) that this idea was questioned.

This picture by Galileo in 1635 shows Aristotle (left) discussing astronomy with Ptolemy (90–160 CE) in the centre and Copernicus (right).

Did you know?

Aristotle is remembered as a great thinker in many areas, but he didn't think much of women. He branded them second-class citizens, unfit for any legal or political rights.

Pioneer of science

Aristotle wrote more than 20[illegible] books. He pioneered the use of logic instead of mysticism, and founded the science of zoology. He also paved the way to the creation of the modern scientific method, which emphasizes observation and experimentation.

At a time when Aristotle was out of favour among Islamic thinkers, **AVERROES** *(1126–1198) defended Aristotle's work and became a great scientist and mathematician.*

The Italian priest **THOMAS AQUINAS** *(1225–1274) built on Aristotle's ideas, and became one of the West's most influential philosophers.*

Karl Marx

The man who thought society should be different, and put the REVOLT into revolting peasants

All about me

■ **BORN:** 1818
■ **DIED:** 1883
■ **NATIONALITY:** German
■ **FACTOID:** I died before my ideas were widely recognized.
■ **IN A NUTSHELL:** I was born in Trier, Germany. I started off as a journalist, but had some radical ideas about how people should live.

Das Kapital

In 1867, Marx published his ideas in the book "Das Kapital".

A new society

Marx believed that **capitalist societies** (where people work to maximize profit) were run by the rich ***for their own benefit***, and the lower classes could only suffer. He came up with an new idea for a classless society. In this type of society, everyone would have a fair share of the goods and wealth produced. This became known as **COMMUNISM**.

The people revolt

Marx's teachings had their first great triumph during the **Russian Revolution**. In 1917, Russia's lower classes ***overthrew the Russian royal family***. The country's new leader, Vladimir Lenin, based his government on Marx's ideas and created a proletarian dictatorship (a country ruled by the lower classes). In 1922, Russia became the **SOVIET UNION**.

All about me

- **BORN:** 1856
- **DIED:** 1939
- **NATIONALITY:** Austrian
- **FACTOID:** The Nazis hated my ideas so much that they burned my books.
- **IN A NUTSHELL:** I was the oldest of eight children, but I'm sure that I was my mother's favourite.

Sigmund Freud

The psychologist that got inside his patients' MINDS, and tried to unlock the mysteries of dreams

The power of dreams

Freud considered dreams to be a window into the mind. He thought that the **subconscious mind** (the part that we are not in control of) uses **SYMBOLS** to represent what a person wants or fears. For example, in a dream, a ***king and queen*** might represent your parents.

Talk therapy

Freud believed that things that happened during a person's childhood ***can have an effect*** on their adult life. He came up with a technique called **PSYCHOANALYSIS**, in which a person would **talk about events** from their past. Freud would then interpret those events to get to the root of the problem.

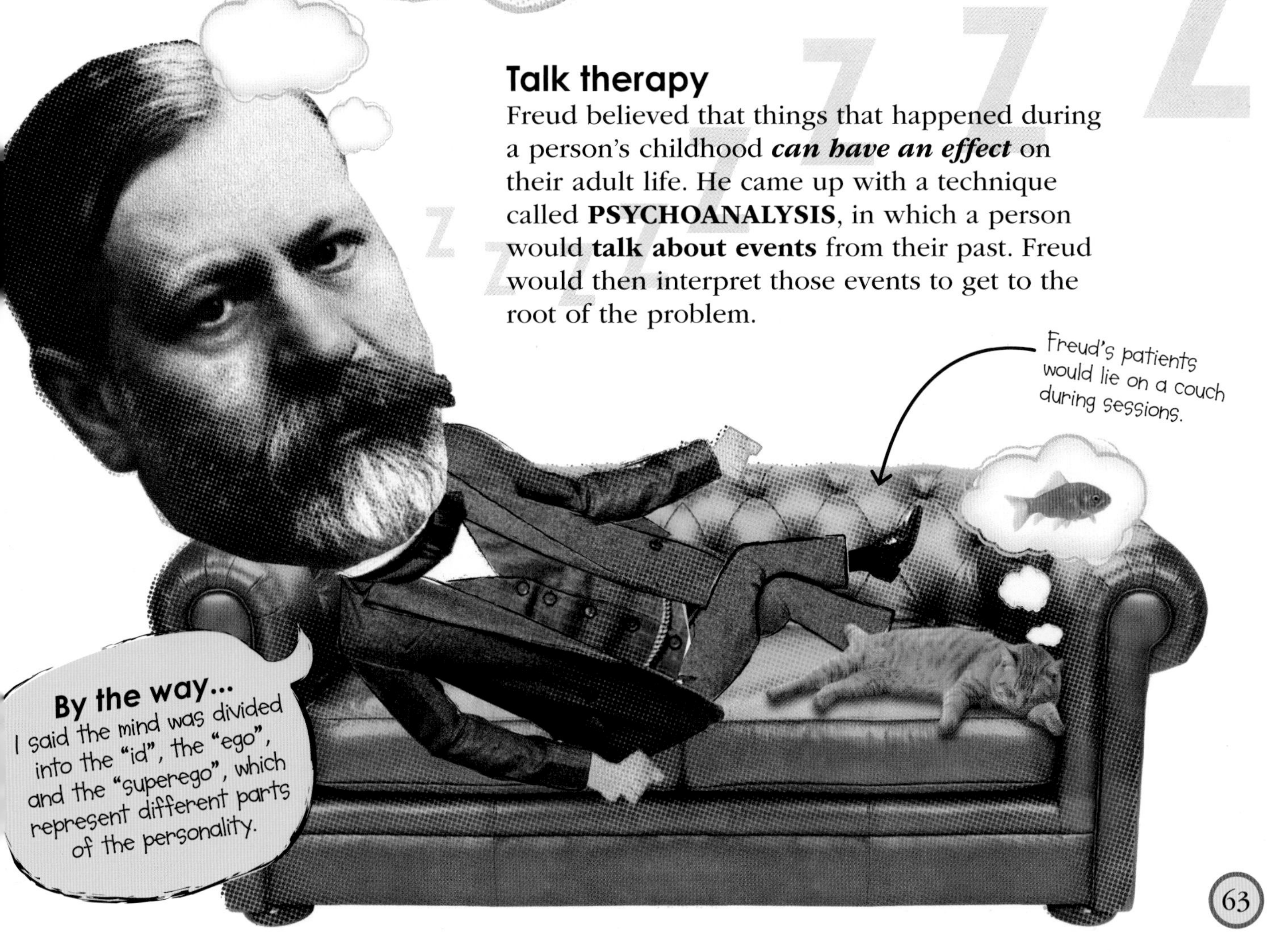

Freud's patients would lie on a couch during sessions.

By the way...
I said the mind was divided into the "id", the "ego", and the "superego", which represent different parts of the personality.

All about me

- **BORN:** 1805
- **DIED:** 1881
- **NATIONALITY:** Jamaican
- **FACTOID:** I was awarded medals by Britain, France, and Turkey.
- **IN A NUTSHELL:** My father was a Scottish soldier and my mother was black, which made me mixed race.

By the way... when I returned to England, I was penniless and sick, so a benefit festival was organized to raise money for me.

Mary Seacole

A pioneering NURSE who, like Florence Nightingale, cared for soldiers in the Crimean War, but got less recognition

The determined nurse

Mary **learned medicine** from her mother, who cared for wounded soldiers. In 1853, when she heard about a ***shortage of nurses*** in the Crimean War, she went to London to volunteer. She was turned down – possibly because of her race – but Mary was certain that she could help, so she travelled to **CRIMEA** (in eastern Europe) anyway.

Medicine

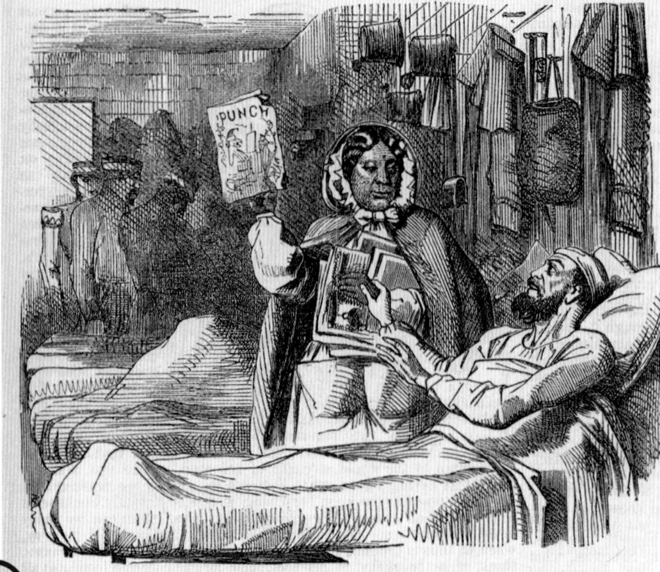

Mother Seacole

With no money, **she built a hospital** with salvaged driftwood, old packing cases, and sheets of iron, which became a ***home for sick soldiers***. During the fighting, she even visited battlefields to nurse the wounded. Her immense **BRAVERY** and nursing skills made her as famous as Nightingale, who looked down on Mary's low social status and mixed-race background. Her patients called her Mother Seacole.

All about me

- **BORN:** 1910
- **DIED:** 1997
- **NATIONALITY:** Albanian
- **FACTOID:** My real name is Agnes Gonxha Bojaxhiu.
- **IN A NUTSHELL:** I heard stories about Christian missionaries as a child and decided that was what I wanted to do.

Mother Teresa

The CATHOLIC NUN who spent 45 years caring for the poor, sick, orphaned, and dying

The Missionaries

Teresa was horrified by the ***poverty and suffering*** she saw on the streets when she was teaching in **Kolkata** (formerly known as Calcutta), India. She started a new order, called the Missionaries of Charity, who took in the sick and dying (including lepers) and cared for them. She also created many **ORPHANAGES**.

International recognition

Teresa's service to humanity drew worldwide recognition. She received **124 awards** for her charitable work and was given the **NOBEL PEACE PRIZE** in 1979. When she died, the Missionaries of Charity had 610 missions in 123 countries, which care for the sick, dying, and orphaned, and ***feed and educate the poor***.

By the way...
I was beatified by Pope John Paul II in 2003, which is the first step to becoming a saint.

By 17, Teresa knew that she wanted to be a nun

Joan of Arc

The TEENAGER who defied the English

Into every battle Joan carried a flag decorated with *Fleur-de-lis*, which, in French, literally translates to "lily flower".

Most teenagers complain about having to tidy their room, but, at the age of 17, Joan took command of the French army and fought against the English.

Peasant girl

Joan of Arc was born in the French hamlet of Domrémy in 1412. Her parents were **peasant farmers** so Joan didn't go to school. When she was nine, her home region was **RAIDED** by the English. From that day on, Joan ***hated*** them.

By the way...
I was once shot in the leg with a crossbow while trying to liberate Paris, but even that wasn't enough to make me leave the battlefield!

Strange visitors

One day, when Joan was just 12, she claimed she was working on her parent's fields when she saw something ***unusual***. Saint Michael, Saint Catherine, and Saint Margaret turned up in the field and told her to **DRIVE THE ENGLISH OUT** of France.

She couldn't have done it without...

The future French king, **CHARLES VII** *(1403–1461) gave Joan command of the French army in 1429.*

Teenage warrior

Not wanting to disobey a **heavenly vision**, Joan talked her way into the French army when she was 17 years old. After persuading the French ruler, the Dauphin Charles, to support her, she was given command of the army, rescued the city of Orléans from an ***English siege***, and went on to lead the army to a series of **SPECTACULAR** victories.

End of the road

Joan's luck ran out when she was ***captured*** in battle at Compiègne and sold to the English. She was put on trial for heresy and found **guilty**. In 1431, at the age of 19, she was **BURNED** at the stake at Rouen, France.

National hero

Even if you don't believe in heavenly visitations, Joan's story is pretty impressive. Her actions helped to give France a sense of national pride, and women all over the world see her as a source of inspiration.

Did you know?
Pope Callixtus III declared that Joan was innocent 25 years after her execution, and then proclaimed her a martyr.

In 1429, the Italian poet **CHRISTINE DE PIZAN** *(1363–c.1430) wrote the first poem about Joan's achievements, adding to Joan's legendary status.*

In 1920, **POPE BENEDICT XV** *(1854–1922) declared Joan of Arc a saint. Today, she is a very popular saint in the Catholic Church.*

Martin Luther King

The champion of race EQUALITY

King was an American clergyman who became the voice of black Americans and the leader of the civil rights movement.

From pastor to protestor

Martin Luther King Jr was born in Atlanta, Georgia, USA, in 1929, and trained to be a ***Baptist minister***. However, in 1955, when a black woman, Rosa Parks, was arrested for **refusing to give up her seat on a bus** to a white man, he took the lead in the **CIVIL RIGHTS MOVEMENT**, and fought for equal rights for black people.

By the way... around 200,000 people turned up at the Lincoln Memorial in Washington DC, USA, to hear me give my famous "I have a dream" speech.

The divided society

America in the 1950s was a time of **RACIAL SEGREGATION**. Many black people were denied the **right to vote**, and were forced to live in separate housing. Signs with messages such as "***coloureds***" ***and "whites only***" were put up in parks, toilets, theatres, and water fountains.

He couldn't have done it without...

The 16th American President **ABRAHAM LINCOLN** *(1809–1865) put an* **END TO SLAVERY** *in America.*

Fighting for a dream

After Rosa Parks was arrested, King led a boycott of the bus system. He organized ***mass protests***, which, although they were peaceful, were attacked, and King was arrested and imprisoned. After being released, he led a **huge march** on Washington in 1963, where he delivered a speech, famous for the words: "**I HAVE A DREAM** that my four little children will one day live in a nation where they will not be judged by the colour of their skin but by the content of their character".

In his speech, King called for an end to discrimination.

King is buried with his wife near his childhood home.

A bitter end

King's ideas were very unpopular among many white Americans. His house was ***firebombed***, and he was arrested **more than 30 times**. On 4 April 1968, he was shot and **KILLED** by an assassin in Memphis, Tennessee, USA. His death set off riots in more than 100 American cities.

King's dream comes true

The march on Washington in 1963, and King's stirring speech, made civil rights something that politicians could no longer ignore. In 1964, race discrimination was made illegal. The same year, King became the youngest person to date to receive the Nobel Peace Prize.

Rosa Parks *(1913–2005) became a symbol of the civil rights movement after she refused to give up her bus seat.*

King was inspired by the peaceful protests, led by **Mahatma Gandhi** *(1869–1948), against British rule of India.*

Religious leaders

New INSIGHTS into the meaning of life

The teachings of the Buddha, Jesus, Muhammad, and Guru Nanak have had a huge impact on human history and the lives of billions of people.

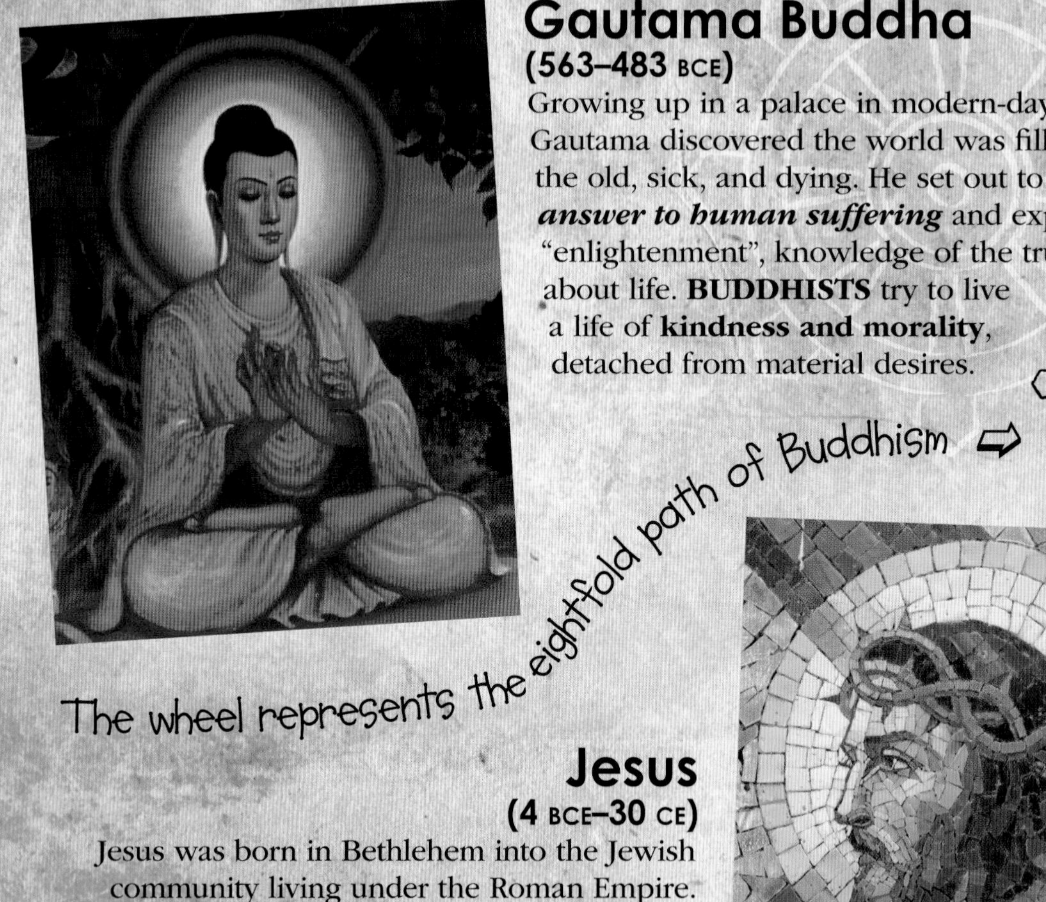

Gautama Buddha

(563–483 BCE)

Growing up in a palace in modern-day Nepal, Gautama discovered the world was filled with the old, sick, and dying. He set out to ***find the answer to human suffering*** and experienced "enlightenment", knowledge of the truth about life. **BUDDHISTS** try to live a life of **kindness and morality**, detached from material desires.

The wheel represents the eightfold path of Buddhism

Jesus

(4 BCE–30 CE)

Jesus was born in Bethlehem into the Jewish community living under the Roman Empire. After his baptism by John the Baptist, he began preaching that the **reign of God** was about to begin. He healed the sick, ***performed wonders***, and taught repentance and forgiveness. He was crucified as a troublemaker by the Roman authorities, but **CHRISTIANS** believe he rose from the dead and lives eternally.

This fish was an early Christian secret symbol

Muhammad
(570–632 CE)

Muhammad grew up in Mecca, in modern-day Saudi Arabia. Muhammad taught that he received the direct word of God (or Allah in Arabic), the ***Qur'an***, from the angel Gabriel, and that he was sent as the **prophet of Allah** to spread the message. Although he faced opposition at first, Muhammad succeeded in gathering a large following, and **ISLAM,** which means "submission to Allah" in Arabic, spread widely throughout the world.

Islam doesn't allow images of Muhammad – this is his name in Arabic.

⇦ The crescent Moon and star is the symbol of Islam

Guru Nanak
(1469–1539 CE)

Guru Nanak was born a Hindu in Nankana, in modern-day Pakistan. Nanak ***sought the truth about God***, and had an experience that he described as being taken to the court of God. From this experience, he set out to teach people that a **profound awareness of God** was more important than the customs of religions. His followers are called "**SIKHS**", which means "disciples".

⇧ The Khanda symbolizes God's universal and creative power

Emmeline Pankhurst

The woman who gave WOMEN a voice

By the way... not every country had to fight like we did. Women were given the vote in New Zealand in 1893, and in 1902 in Australia.

At a time when women should be seen and not heard, Emmeline Pankhurst got herself seen, and she was certainly heard.

A fighting start

Emmeline was born in 1858 in Manchester, England. Her family had a history of **RADICAL POLITICS**, and her husband, Richard Pankhurst, a supporter of ***women's rights***, wrote an act of parliament that allowed married women to keep their own property.

Taking a stand

In 1889, Emmeline founded the Women's Franchise League, who **campaigned for women** to have the right to vote in local elections. In 1903, Pankhurst helped to create the more aggressive Women's Social and Political Union (WSPU). The WSPU soon had a ***reputation for radical activities***. Its members were given the nickname "**SUFFRAGETTES**" as a joke by a newspaper.

The suffragette colours were purple (for dignity), white (for purity), and green (for hope).

She couldn't have done it without...

Nicholas de Codorcet *(1743–1794) and* **Olympe de Gouges** *(1748–1793) argued for women's rights in France.*

The English writer **Mary Wollstonecraft** *(1759–1797) argued that women were not inferior to men.*

Votes for Women

A tough battle

Anything could happen when suffragettes demonstrated – they smashed windows, set fire to buildings, and held **hunger strikes**. Emmeline was **ARRESTED MANY TIMES** and went on hunger strike herself. In one protest, in 1913, a suffragette named Emily Davison was killed when she ***threw herself under the king's horse*** during a race.

Success at last

During the First World War, Britain's men were away fighting, so **women had to take on their jobs**. In 1918, women over 30 were finally given **THE RIGHT TO VOTE**. Ten years later, just after Emmeline's death, they were allowed to vote at age 21, which was the same age as men.

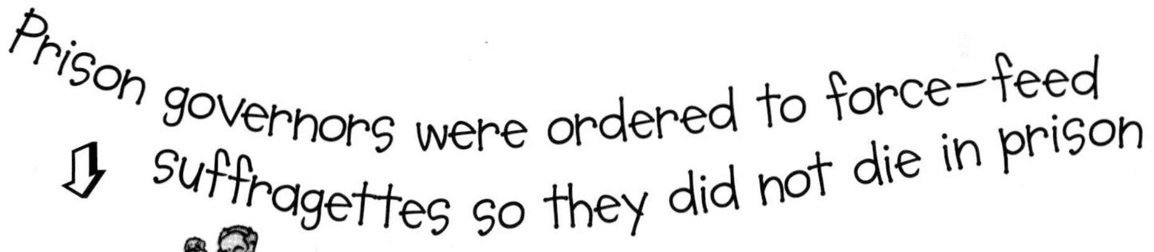

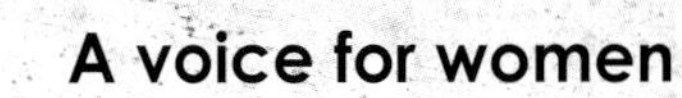

A voice for women

Emmeline Pankhurst, and others like her, made sure that women have the same rights as men. Today, every woman in Britain has the right to vote at the age of 18. Women in the USA were given the same rights in 1920.

KATE SHEPPARD *(1847–1934) led the call for women's suffrage in New Zealand, the first country to give it.*

The American campaigner **SUSAN B ANTHONY** *(1820–1906) travelled the world giving speeches about women's rights.*

Eleanor Roosevelt

The social CAMPAIGNER who is one of the most influential women of the 20th century

All about me

- **BORN:** 1884
- **DIED:** 1962
- **NATIONALITY:** American
- **FACTOID:** My husband was President of the United States.
- **IN A NUTSHELL:** At 15, I was sent to finishing school near London, England, where my headmistress taught me the importance of independent thinking.

Eleanor wrote her popular newspaper columnn, "My Day", from 1935 to 1962.

A first lady with a heart

Eleanor's husband, Franklin, was America's President from 1933 to 1945. During this time, she discussed her concerns and opinions in a **newspaper column**. She helped to create the **NATIONAL YOUTH ADMINISTRATION** (NYA), which helped young people – male and female – get training. During the Second World War she helped gather civilian volunteers and ***visited American troops abroad***.

By the way... people wanted me to run for Vice President with President Truman in 1948, but I wasn't interested.

Eleanor with the members of the Commission on Human Rights in 1946.

The UN ambassador

In 1946, Eleanor became the first chairperson of the ***United Nations (UN) Human Rights Commission***. Two years later, she helped create the "**UNIVERSAL DECLARATION OF HUMAN RIGHTS**", which stated that everyone was entitled to the same freedoms and rights. She also supported the foundation of the State of Israel, and tried to **open negotiations** with the Soviet Union during the Cold War, a time of great political hostility between the Soviet Union and the United States.

All about me

BORN: 1945
NATIONALITY: Burmese
FACTOID: I won the Nobel Peace Prize in 1991.
ANOTHER FACTOID: My father, Aung San, was assassinated after helping to negotiate Burma's independence from Britain in 1947.
IN A NUTSHELL: I was born in Rangoon, Burma. I studied at Oxford University in England, then became a housewife in London.

The fighting peacock on the NLD flag is a symbol of protest against the military government.

A symbol of hope

In 1988, Suu Kyi returned to Burma from her home in London to care for her mother. At the time, the country was **torn apart by violence**. The people were ***demanding democracy***, but the ruling military party was using the army against them. Suu Kyi dared to stand up at a rally and **CALL FOR FREEDOM**.

By the way... when my husband died in Britain in 1999, I couldn't attend his funeral for fear of not being let back into Burma.

Under house arrest

The same year (1988), she helped found the ***National League for Democracy*** (NLD), but a new military party (junta) had taken over and they placed Suu Kyi under **HOUSE ARREST** in 1989. Even though she couldn't attend, the NLD easily won the country's first election for 30 years, but **the junta refused to give up their powe**r, and Suu Kyi remained under house arrest until 2010.

Aung San Suu Kyi

The woman who fought for FREEDOM for the people of Burma

Jane Goodall

The champion of the CHIMPS

Jane Goodall spent 45 years studying chimpanzees in the wild, showing the world that chimps are far more like us than anyone before had imagined.

Out of Africa

Jane Goodall was born in London, England, in 1934. From a young age, she **DREAMED OF WORKING WITH ANIMALS** in the wild. At just 26 she travelled to Gombe National Park in East Africa to study chimpanzees. The palaeontologist Louis Leakey funded Goodall's research, noting her **observational skills and patience**.

By the way...
unlike most researchers, I gave all my chimps names. Other scientists just give them a number, so they don't get too attached.

Meet the family

At first, Goodall had a very difficult time ***interacting with the chimps*** and they often fled when she approached them. However, after a few months, the chimps started to **ACCEPT HER PRESENCE** in their world.

She couldn't have done it without...

JOHN MUIR *(1838–1914) was an American adventurer and conservationist who set up the first* **NATIONAL PARKS** *in the United States.*

Amazing discoveries

After many years watching and studying chimps, Jane realized how **similar they are to humans**. She saw that they have a social structure, look after their friends, and even go to war. She also witnessed chimps **CREATING TOOLS** from rocks, twigs, branches, stems, and leaves.

These young chimpanzees are trying to make tools using rocks and twigs.

Monkey business

To help protect her hairy friends, in 1977 she founded the **Jane Goodall Institute for Wildlife Research, Education and Conservation**. The group was set up to continue research into wild chimpanzees and to **PROTECT THEIR HOMES.**

A vet examines a protected chimpanzee on Ngamba Island, Uganda, a sanctuary associated with the Jane Goodall Institute.

Great apes

Jane's work is now the longest continuous study of any animal in the wild. She has shown us how chimps have personalities, live in complex societies, and that they are not so very different to you and me.

Did you know?

Chimps use chewed up leaves as a sponge to soak up water, and use twigs as tools to reach tasty bugs.

An early promoter of **GLOBAL CONSERVATION** *was the American marine biologist* **RACHEL CARSON** *(1907–1964).*

The American zoologist **DIAN FOSSEY** *(1932–1985) studied* **MOUNTAIN GORILLAS**, *and was dedicated to protecting them.*

Leading

Leaders

This group made their mark by leading the pack. Some had a thirst for battle, power, and glory, and won great empires and riches. Others kicked out their rulers because they thought they could do a better job. But they didn't all want to start a fight; a few just wanted peace and equality. Whether monarchs or generals or freedom fighters, these leaders were all very good at telling other people what to do.

Alexander the Great

The UNSTOPPABLE conquering machine

In just 10 years, Alexander crushed the mighty Persian Empire, founded more than 70 cities, and created a empire more than 5 million sq km (2 million sq miles) in total size.

The impatient king

Alexander was born in the Greek kingdom of Macedon in 356 BCE. His father, King Phillip II, was **assassinated** in 336 BCE and so, at the age of 20, ***Alexander became king***. After crushing a Greek uprising (they didn't much like Macedonian barbarians), he set off to conquer the huge **PERSIAN EMPIRE**.

By the way... my eyes were different colours – one was blue, and the other was brown.

He couldn't have done it without...

PHILLIP II *(382–336 BCE) transformed Macedon into a great power,* **REVOLUTIONIZED THE ARMY**, *and made his son's conquests possible.*

Alexander's tutor **ARISTOTLE** *(384–322 BCE) wrote a book called* **ON KINGSHIP** *to try to teach his pupil how to be a good ruler.*

The war machine

Alexander led his army to one victory after another. They swept across Asia Minor, Syria, and Egypt before finally defeating the Persian king, Darius, at the **Battle of Gaugamela** in 331 BCE. At the age of 25, Alexander was ***king of Macedonia***, leader of the Greeks, overlord of Asia Minor, pharaoh of Egypt and "**GREAT KING**" of Persia. This map shows Alexander's empire at its peak.

EUROPE
ASIA
MACEDON
THRACE
Troy
Athens
Sardis
Halicarnassus
Tarsus
ASSYRIA
Nineveh
MEDIA
PARTHIA
BACTRIA
Bactra
Samarkand
Mediterranean Sea
Tyre
Gaza
Alexandria
Siwa
Memphis
EGYPT
MESOPOTAMIA
Babylon
Susa
Pasargadae
Persepolis
GEDROSIA
Pura
Pattala
Arabian Sea
AFRICA

The legend

Alexander was surrounded by many **MYTHS AND LEGENDS**. One legend says that he heard of a prophecy that foretold that whoever untied the (impossible) **Gordian knot** would rule all of Asia. Alexander's solution was to simply hack through the knot with his sword. Another myth says he was the ***son of Zeus***.

Did you know?
Alexander founded or renamed more than 70 cities – many of them were called "Alexandria", after himself.

Master strategist

Alexander was a **BRILLIANT GENERAL**. At the Battle of Issus in 333 BCE, his ***40,000 nen faced 100,000 Persians*** on ground that suited the nemy. Even though Alexander was wounded, **his army won he day**, and the Persian king, Darius III, had to flee.

West meets East

Alexander died when he was just 32. However, his legacy includes a vast empire that spread western culture as far as India, and opened trade routes that would last for centuries.

BUCEPHALUS *(355–326 BCE) was Alexander's war horse, which he rode to some of his greatest victories. When he died, Alexander named a city,* **BUCEPHALIA**, *after him.*

PTOLEMY *(323–282 BCE) was Alexander's close childhood friend and* **LOYAL GENERAL**. *When Alexander died, Ptolemy became pharaoh of Egypt.*

Augustus Caesar

The first EMPEROR of Rome

As Rome's first emperor, Augustus had brushed aside hundreds of years of the Roman republican tradition and replaced it with a peaceful monarchy.

Young warrior

Augustus was originally called Octavian, and was born in Rome in 63 BCE. When his great-uncle ***Julius Caesar*** was assassinated in 44 BCE, his will named Augustus as his heir. Although he was only 18, Augustus raised an army and **defeated Caesar's assassins**. He then defeated his former ally, Mark Anthony, and **TOOK CONTROL OF ROME**.

Augustus used coins to spread his image.

First citizen of Rome

Romans hated the idea of being ruled by a king, so Augustus didn't make the same mistake as Julius, who became dictator and claimed ***total power for himself.*** Instead, Augustus called himself the "**FIRST CITIZEN**". He reorganized Rome's army, and made it more permanent. This ensured that he **stayed in control**, and also allowed him to expand the Roman Empire.

He couldn't have done it without...

ROME WAS FOUNDED IN 753 BCE. *According to legend it was established by the twin brothers* **ROMULUS AND REMUS.**

In 509 BCE, **LUCIUS JUNIUS BRUTUS** *led the overthrow of Rome's king, Lucius Tarquinius Superbus, and* **FOUNDED THE REPUBLIC.**

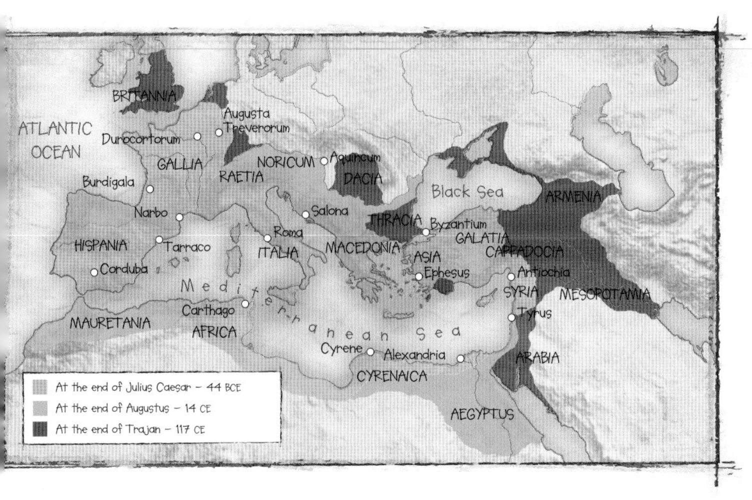

The empire builders

By Julius Caesar's death in 44 BCE, the Roman Empire covered most of the Mediterranean, France, and some of Spain. ***Augustus made it much bigger***, and, by 14 CE, he had added Egypt, the rest of Spain, and large parts of central Europe. He tried to **invade Germany**, but was met by barbarian hordes and it turned out to be a disaster. The empire reached its peak under **EMPEROR TRAJAN** in 117 CE.

By the way...
my real name is Gaius Octavius, but I changed it to Augustus Caesar. All future emperors would be known as "Caesar", or "Augustus".

Remodelling Rome

After decades of civil war, ***Rome was a mess***, so Augustus set about rebuilding it. He built many new temples, including the famous "**PANTHEON**" (pictured right), and rebuilt almost every major building in Rome. He also restored the city's **sewer and water systems**.

The greatest emperor

Many consider Augustus to be Rome's greatest emperor. He reformed the Roman tax system, developed networks of roads with an efficient postal service, and created police and fire-fighting services. His reign laid the foundations for an empire that lasted for 1,500 years.

The great general **JULIUS CAESAR** *(100–44 BCE) set the wheels in motion for the end of the Roman Republic by becoming* **DICTATOR**.

MARK ANTONY *(83–30 BCE)* **HELPED AUGUSTUS WIN THE CIVIL WAR** *against Julius Caesar's assassins, Brutus and Cassius.*

Charlemagne

The "father of modern EUROPE"

As king of the Franks and Christian emperor of the West, Charlemagne laid the foundations of modern Europe. That's why he's also known as Charles the Great.

The man who would be king

Charlemagne was born in 747 near Liège in modern-day Belgium. He was the son of the Frankish king **Pepin the Short**. Pepin died in 768 and left his kingdom to Charlemagne and his brother, Carloman. When his **BROTHER DIED** suddenly in 771, Charlemagne became ***sole ruler*** of the Franks.

Charlemagne personally led 53 campaigns and took part in hundreds of battles.

By the way...
before me, people wrote in capital letters. I introduced lower-case letters, called Carolingian script, which is easier to read.

The Christian soldier

In 773, Pope Hadrian I asked for Charlemagne's help to **defend the Papal States** from invaders. He saw off the **POPE'S ENEMIES** and was named "protector of the Church". In his position as Papal protector, he ***fought against the Muslims*** in northern Spain, and conquered large parts of Germany, Switzerland, Austria, and Belgium.

Charlemagne the wise

Charlemagne organized a new system of ***governors*** to keep order throughout his kingdom. In additon, he used inspectors to keep an eye on the governors. He also improved **COMMERCE** by standardizing **weights and measures** (so people were guaranteed to always get the correct weight).

He devised the monetary system of pounds, shillings, and pence.

He couldn't have done it without...

Charlemagne defended **POPE LEO III** *(750–816) from a rebellion in 800, so the Pope declared him* **EMPEROR OF THE ROMANS**.

The Frankish scholar **EINHARD** *(775–840) wrote a* **BIOGRAPHY** *of Charlemagne, which recorded his life and achievements in history.*

Charlemagne's crown was used in the coronation of every French king until 1722.

The great teacher

Charlemagne was appalled by how few people in France were able to **read and write** – even many of the country's priests were illiterate. He called in **SCHOLARS** from Britain and Ireland to restore the schools of France. He also organized a school at his royal palace at Aachen (in modern-day Germany), and introduced ***monastic schools*** all over Europe.

Charlemagne would visit his new schools to make sure they reached his standards.

Shaping Europe

Charlemagne took a group of squabbling and separate Frankish kingdoms and laid the foundations for the unified country of France. His empire encouraged the emergence of a more enlightened and better educated Europe.

He paved the way for...

Charlemagne saw himself as the heir to the **ROMAN EMPIRE** *when he was crowned emperor in 800. His successors became known as* **HOLY ROMAN EMPERORS**, *and the title survived until 1805.*

NAPOLEON *(1769–1821) wanted to recreate Charlemagne's military and administrative achievements by creating a "modern"* **FRENCH EMPIRE**.

Cool queens

LADIES who lorded it

Many queens were overshadowed by their king, but every so often a queen stepped out of the shadows and became a legend.

Hatshepsut
(1508–1458 BCE)

There was nothing average about this **Egyptian oddity**. She married her half-brother, the pharaoh Thutmose II. He died very young, so Hatshepsut declared that she would be the new **PHARAOH**. She dressed as a man and ***even wore a false beard***, but, under her almost 22-years as ruler, Egypt flourished.

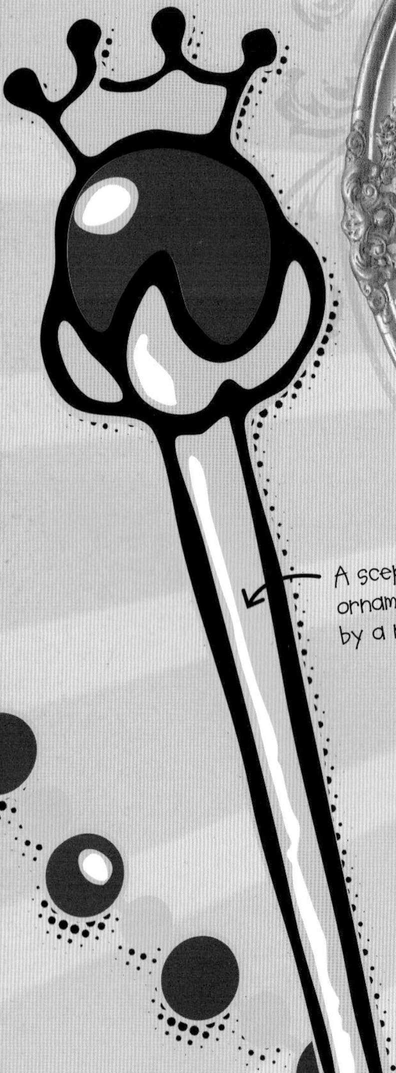

A sceptre is an ornamental rod held by a ruling monarch.

Cleopatra
(69–30 BCE)

This **EGYPTIAN QUEEN** was as deadly as she was **beautiful**. She seduced the Roman general, Julius Caesar, and convinced him to ***get rid of the pharaoh***, who was her brother and her husband. Then, she used another Roman, Mark Anthony, to kill her sister.

France has never been ruled by a queen

Maria Teresa

(1717–1780)

Maria became **EMPRESS OF THE AUSTRIAN EMPIRE** when her father, Charles VI, died. She reorganized Austria's army, and **introduced compulsory schooling**, which brought the flagging empire back to life. She had ***16 children***, which included two queens, a few duchesses, and two Holy Roman Emperors.

Catherine the Great

(1729–1796)

To become "great" this **RUSSIAN QUEEN** first got rid of her husband, the Emperor of Russia, Peter III. She then **increased the amount of land controlled by Russia**, and promoted education and the new philosophy of ***"enlightened" thinking***. Unfortunately, all this only helped the rich, so the poor probably didn't think she was that great at all.

Queen Victoria

(1819–1901)

Victoria was only 18 when she became **QUEEN AND EMPRESS OF THE BRITISH EMPIRE**. She might have been short, but for 64 years she ***ruled more than 450 million people*** in an empire that covered a quarter of the globe. Her 42 grandchildren occupied the thrones of most of Europe, earning her the nickname "**the grandmother of Europe**".

Genghis Khan

The greatest CONQUEROR the world has ever seen

In just 25 years, Genghis Khan conquered more lands and people than Alexander the Great and Napoleon combined.

A tough start

Genghis was born in 1162, and his father, Yesugei, was a local **tribal chief**. After his father was killed, his family was forced into **HIDING** and had to scrape a living on the ***Mongolian plains***.

Hit and run

The Mongol army **relied on their horses** and the element of surprise. Their skilled **MOUNTED ARCHERS** would ride at the enemy, ***fire a volley of arrows***, and then ride off again. A Mongol army could travel more than 60 km (100 miles) in a day.

By the way... my real name was Temujin. The name Genghis, which means "sea", was given to me after I became chief, or Khan.

Archers fired when their horse had all its legs off the ground to avoid bumps ruining their shots.

Mongol horses were equipped with stirrups, which gave their riders much more control.

He couldn't have done it without...

Toghrul *(died 1203) was a close friend of Genghis's father. He adopted Genghis and made him his* **HEIR**.

Ögedei Khan *(1186–1241) was Genghis's third son and* **SUCCESSOR**. *He expanded the Mongol Empire.*

The great conqueror

After ***years in the wilderness***, Genghis took back his father's tribe and united the Mongol tribes. By 1204, Genghis was **SUPREME KHAN** of all the Mongols, and was ready for war. Within five years, his army had taken parts of China. They then took Siberia, Afghanistan, and parts of the Persian Empire. Cities were so **afraid of the Khan** that they often surrendered before he even arrived.

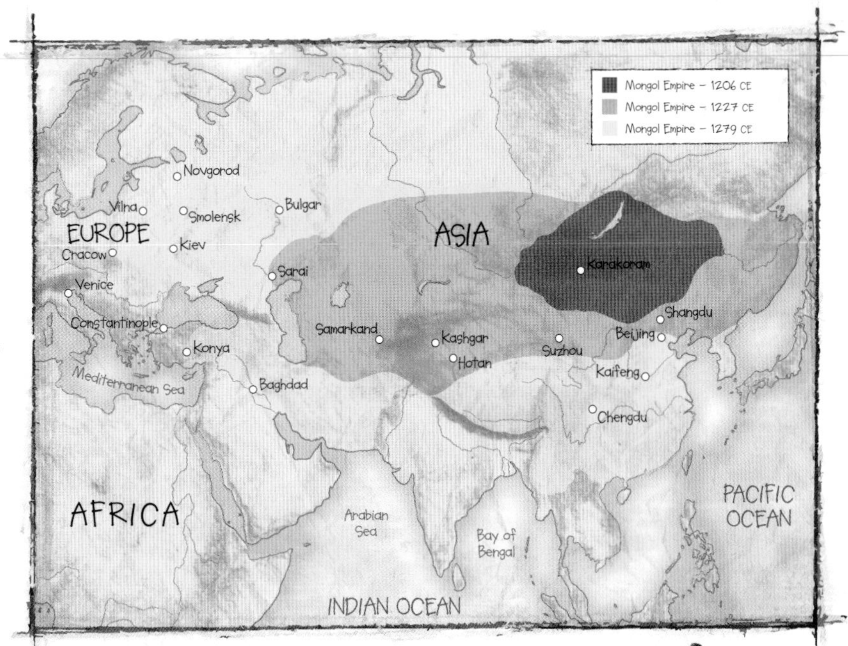

Mongols lived in "gers" (meaning "home"), which were circular wooden frames covered with felt.

War on the move

Every Mongol warrior usually owned three or four horses, which they kept roped together. By frequently changing horses, the army could cover **huge distances very quickly**. The Mongols were **NOMADIC**, so they were used to travelling around. At the end of the day they would build camp and practise their battle skills by ***hunting for their dinner***.

A mighty empire

Genghis created the world's longest lasting empire. He encouraged religious tolerance, introduced new laws, and brought a new writing system to the illiterate Mongol people. Unfortunately, up to 40 million people might have died as a result of his conquests.

He paved the way for...

Genghis's grandson **KUBLAI KHAN** *(1215–1294) established the Yuan Dynasty and became* **EMPEROR OF CHINA**.

DNA STUDIES *have shown that as many as* **16 MILLION MEN** *worldwide are descended from Genghis Khan.*

Saladin

The man who took JERUSALEM from the Crusaders

Saladin was a great Muslim leader who retook the Holy Land and who, despite his fearsome reputation, treated his enemies with respect.

In Arabic, Saladin means "Righteousness of faith"

The young warrior

Saladin was born in Mesopotamia (modern-day Iraq) in 1138. As a young man, he helped his uncle, a general for the Sultan of Syria, win a **great victory against the Crusaders**. His uncle became ruler of Egypt and, when he died, ***Saladin took power*** for himself.

The name "Crusaders" comes from "crux" (Latin for cross) because they carried the cross with them as a symbol.

A clash of religions

Jerusalem was a very important city to **Jews, Christians, and Muslims**. For centuries, its Arab rulers had allowed Christian and Jewish ***pilgrims*** into the city. However, by 1095, the Muslim rulers of Jerusalem were making travel to the city more difficult for pilgrims. The crusades were started by the Christians to **RETAKE JERUSALEM**.

He couldn't have done it without...

Muslims believe that **MUHAMMAD** *(570–632) ascended to heaven at* **DOME OF THE ROCK**. *Saladin used the Dome as a symbol to unite the Arabs to his cause.*

Saladin's revenge

In 1097, before Saladin was born, the Crusaders had captured Jerusalem, killing many of its inhabitants, and taken control of the Holy Land. Saladin was determined to retake it for Muslims, and he declared **a holy war** against the Crusaders. In 1187, with a huge army, Saladin **CRUSHED HIS ENEMIES** at the Battle of Hattin, and the Crusader King of Jerusalem, Guy of Lusignan, was forced to surrender (pictured right). ***Saladin retook Jerusalem***, but, unlike the Crusaders, he allowed its inhabitants to leave the city peacefully.

By the way...
when I heard that Richard the Lionheart had a fever, I sent him peaches, pears, and ice from the top of Mount Hermon, 160 km (100 miles) away.

Chivalrous knight
In the Muslim world, Saladin is remembered as the man who united the Arab people and liberated Jerusalem. Even in Europe, Saladin was revered as a chivalrous knight – in fact, an epic poem was written about his exploits.

The Crusaders strike back

In 1189, England's king, ***Richard the Lionheart***, led the Third Crusade. They retook the city of Acre, but the siege took two years, and the other kings returned home. Richard couldn't beat Saladin alone, so they **MADE PEACE**. Christians were allowed to visit Jerusalem again, but **their rule of the Holy Land had ended for good**.

Did you know?
After a lifetime of campaigning, Saladin left an empire stretching north from Egypt, but he died almost penniless.

In 1183, Saladin captured the strategically important **CITADEL OF ALEPPO**. *It was a crucial step on his way to retaking Jerusalem*

IBN SHADDAD *(1145–1234) wrote a biography about Saladin called* **THE RARE AND EXCELLENT HISTORY OF SALADIN**.

Martin Luther

The man who SPLIT the church in two

Martin Luther was a German priest who challenged the Catholic Church.

Struck by God

Martin Luther was born in 1483 in Eisleben, Germany. His parents wanted him to be a lawyer, so he studied law at university. One day he was almost **struck by lightning** during a storm. He thought that the close call was a **SIGN FROM GOD** that he should leave law, and he joined a monastery.

Luther nailed his *95 Theses* to the door of the church in Wittenberg, Germany.

Forgiveness for sale

Luther soon realized that the Catholic Church was pretty corrupt. Priests were selling "**INDULGENCES**", which were a sort of "get-out-of-jail-free" card for sinners to get into heaven. In 1517, Luther wrote a list of complaints relating to the Catholic Church, which he called his ***95 Theses***. His **ideas spread** around Europe very quickly.

Summoned by the Pope

Pope Leo X didn't take kindly to Luther's meddling, so he summoned Luther to the "**DIET OF WORMS**" – a Diet was a sort of meeting, and Worms was the town it was held in (no worms were eaten!) In 1521, Luther was declared an ***outlaw*** and heretic.

He couldn't have done it without...

In 1440, the **PRINTING PRESS** *made it possible for Luther's ideas to reach a lot of people very quickly.*

DESIDERIUS ERASMUS ROTERODAMUS *(1466–1536) was a Dutch priest who also questioned the Catholic Church.*

By the way...
I had a fairly low opinion of myself. I even said that "I am but a stinking bag of worms". Hug, anyone?

A Bible for everyone

Heretics were **burned at the stake**. Luther didn't want to be burned, so he went into hiding. In 1534, he ***translated the Bible*** from Latin into German so everyone would have the chance to read it. He even wrote a sort of **CHILDREN'S VERSION** that parents could use to teach their kids about faith.

Lutheranism is still widely practised today

A church divided

From Christianity's early days, it had been dominated by the Catholic Church. As Luther's writings spread around Europe, more people started to question the Catholic Church. His ideas eventually split Christianity in two, and created a new church called Protestantism, which was named after Luther's protest, and led to a century of religious warfare in Europe. His new translation of the Bible gave normal people access to the church's teachings, and encouraged the spread of literacy.

Did you know?
Luther even insisted that, when he died, all his books and writings should be burned... they weren't.

He paved the way for...

The French priest **JOHN CALVIN** *(1509–1564) created his own branch of Protestantism called Calvinism.*

Luther's translation paved the way for versions of **THE BIBLE** *translated in every country of the world.*

Up the revolution

Rising up AGAINST the establishment!

The guillotine became a symbol of the French Revolution

Maximilien Robespierre

(1758–1794)

This **French politician** hated the aristocracy and everything they stood for, so in 1791 he became one of the leaders of the French Revolution and **CHOPPED OFF THEIR HEADS** (including the king and queen's). His period of power was known as the "Reign of Terror" because he sent around 30,000 people to the ***guillotine***.

Is your king crushing your freedom? Is your government just plain useless? If so, you need to start a revolution... but who should lead it?

Bolívar's famous sword has become an iconic symbol

Simón Bolívar

(1783–1830)

In South America, there aren't many people more famous than Simón Bolívar. As a military and political leader, he managed to **kick the Spanish Empire out** of Venezuela, Bolivia, Columbia, Peru, Ecuador, and Panama. This didn't make him very ***popular*** with Spanish royalty, but he is regarded as a **HERO** all across Latin America.

By the way... after I died, my body was embalmed and put in a glass coffin. To this day it's still on display in Moscow's Red Square.

Vladimir Lenin
(1870–1924)

As leader of the **Bolsheviks**, Lenin was a follower of the Communist ideals of Karl Marx. In 1917, he led the **RUSSIAN REVOLUTION**, overthrew the royal family (who were later killed), and became the first leader of the new communist state, the ***Soviet Union***.

Mao Tse-Tung
(1893–1976)

Another Communist icon, Mao led the ***Red Army*** to victory over the Nationalists in 1949, and established the **PEOPLE'S REPUBLIC OF CHINA**. Ruthless and ambitious, in his first four years in power, he was responsible for the deaths of nearly 1.5 million people. Despite this, he was loved in China for making the country a **modern power**.

Almost every man in China wore a suit like Chairman Mao's ⇨

Fidel Castro
(1926–)

Castro's first attempt to ***overthrow*** Cuba's dictator Fulgencio Batista ended with him being exiled to Mexico. After he teamed up with another revolutionary, Argentinian **CHE GUEVARA** (1928–1967), he led the successful Communist party in **Cuba** from 1956 to 1959. The CIA spent almost 50 years trying to overthrow him (they failed).

Napoleon Bonaparte

The man who CONQUERED Europe

With his many successes on the battlefield, Napoleon was a military genius who soon had the whole of Europe looking up to him.

A fighting start

Napoleon was born in Corsica, France, in 1769. He went to a **MILITARY ACADEMY** in Paris, where he was teased for his Corsican accent and his provincial manners. However, with his **leadership skills**, Napoleon became an artillery officer when he was just 16, and ***rose quickly through the ranks***.

By the way...
I was condemned by Pope Pius VII when I took over the part of Italy that the Catholic Church ruled, so I threw him in prison, where he died.

Zero to hero

During the early years of the **FRENCH REVOLUTION** (1789–1799), when France broke free of its Imperial rule, Napoleon became a **national hero**. In 1799, he led a ***plot to overthrow*** the revolutionary government, and he became the First Consul of France.

He couldn't have done it without...

MAXIMILIEN ROBESPIERRE *(1758–1794) led the French Revolution, got rid of the royal family, and helped create the* **FRENCH REPUBLIC**.

CHARLEMAGNE *(742–814) brought together the separate Frankish kingdoms and created France as* **A SINGLE COUNTRY**.

Emperor of Europe

Napoleon set out to conquer other countries and, in 1804, he crowned himself **EMPEROR**. Soon every country surrounding France (except Britain) was part of his empire. In 1812, he tried to conquer Russia, but it ended in disaster and he was ***sent into exile*** off the coast of Italy. He returned to France and seized power again, but was beaten by Britain at the **Battle of Waterloo** in 1815. Sent into exile again – to the South Atlantic island of St Helena – Napoleon died in 1821.

Legal eagle

In 1804, Napoleon replaced the old French legal system with a new **NAPOLEONIC CODE** of laws. The old system was based on local feudal laws and was **old fashioned and confusing**. The new system was much ***clearer and fairer***.

CODE CIVIL DES FRANÇAIS, MIS EN VERS, Avec le texte en regard. LIVRE PREMIER.

AVIS DE L'ÉDITEUR.

A PARIS,

In just eight years, Napoleon managed to conquer most of Europe.

Lasting impression

Napoleon's reforms brought stability back to France, which had been torn apart by the French Revolution. Many of the laws of his Napoleonic code (above) are still used in France and form the basis of the legal systems of many of the countries that Napoleon conquered.

An essay on MILITARY TACTICS *by the French general* JACQUES ANTOINE HIPPOLYTE *(1743–1790) greatly influenced Napoleon.*

Napoleon was inspired by the military tactics and DOMESTIC REFORMS *of the German Emperor* FREDERICK THE GREAT *(1712–1786).*

George Washington

The first PRESIDENT of the United States

George Washington helped to kick the British out of America. He became a national hero, the first President of the United States of America, and got his face on a lot of coins and banknotes.

The wily woodsman

Washington was born in 1732 in Westmoreland County, Virginia, USA. His father died when he was 11, and he had very **little formal schooling**, but George taught himself to be a woodsman, surveyor, and mapmaker. This all came in useful when, at 20, he joined the **VIRGINIA MILITIA** who, at the time, were fighting for the British (who ruled much of America) ***against the French and their Native American allies***.

On Christmas Day 1776, Washington led his troops across the icy Delaware River, where he surprised and defeated the British. It was a major turning point of the Revolutionary War.

The crafty commander

When the British won the war, they raised taxes to pay for it. This was very unpopular, so on **4 July 1776, the Americans declared independence** and went to war with Britain. Washington was commander of the Continental Army in the **REVOLUTIONARY WAR** and, knowing he could never beat the British in a pitched battle, ordered his troops to attack quickly and then withdraw to safety. By using ***clever tactics***, he was able to defeat the British.

He couldn't have done it without...

Merchant and statesman **JOHN HANCOCK** *(1737–1793) was the first person to sign the* **DECLARATION OF INDEPENDENCE**.

By the way... after the American Revolution, I became so popular that some people wanted to make me King of America.

Washington had spring-loaded false teeth made of cow's teeth and ivory.

The first president

On 19 October 1781, the **British surrendered** at Yorktown, Virginia. The Americans had won their independence, but still had to figure out how to run the country. In the beginning they struggled, but, in 1787, Washington helped to write the **US CONSTITUTION**, which organized the government. In 1789, he was unanimously elected the **first President of the United States**.

Father of a country

Washington played such a big role in the founding of the United States, that he is often called the "Father of his Country". To Americans he is a military and revolutionary hero, and a man of great integrity, duty, and honour. He is celebrated in many ways, including a carving on Mount Rushmore.

PAUL REVERE *(1735–1818) helped organize an* **ALARM SYSTEM** *to keep watch on the British military.*

ALEXANDER HAMILTON *(1757–1804) was a lawyer who helped Washington design the United States' first government.*

Mahatma Gandhi

The man who DEFIED an empire

Gandhi, an icon of peaceful resistance, pioneered non-violent methods of protest against the British government in India. He is known as the "Father of India".

Early struggles

Mohandas Gandhi (known as **Mahatma** or "*great soul*") was born on 2 October 1869 in Porbandar, India. He studied law in London, UK, and then spent 20 years in South Africa, joining the struggle for **BASIC RIGHTS** for Indian immigrants. He was ***arrested many times***, before the government gave in to his demands. When Gandhi returned to India, he found that the British, who had ruled India as a colony since 1858, had passed strict laws to control the Indian population.

By the way... I believe that reacting to violence with more violence is foolish. In a speech, I once said "an eye for an eye makes the whole world blind".

Did you know? When Gandhi died, he owned only 10 possessions including a watch, sandals, spectacles, and an eating bowl.

He paved the way for...

American civil rights activist **MARTIN LUTHER KING** *(1929–1968) campaigned against* **RACIAL INEQUALITIES** *using Gandhi's non-violent methods.*

NELSON MANDELA *(1918–) led the struggle in South Africa to end* **APARTHEID**, *laws that kept people separate based on race. He became South Africa's first black president.*

A powerful peace

In protest against British rule in India, Gandhi started a *satyagraha*, a non-violent method of **PROTEST** that included not obeying harsh laws, boycotting British companies, and living as simple a life as possible. Gandhi attracted ***millions of followers*** and, in 1930, he led 50,000 people marching to the sea in protest against a new salt tax. He spent six years in prison and held a 21-day hunger strike. His ultimate aim was **Indian freedom** and self-rule.

A bitter victory

In 1947, Gandhi won and India was granted ***independence*** from Britain. But the British split the country into two, **divided along religious lines** into Muslim Pakistan and Hindu India. This was very unpopular and **RIOTS** spread across the area. Gandhi tried to bring calm, but he was assassinated in 1948.

Path to peace

Though his life was cut short, Gandhi accomplished a great deal. He helped to gain independence for the land he loved and end many injustices against his people. He spoke of peace, and his life inspired many who came after him.

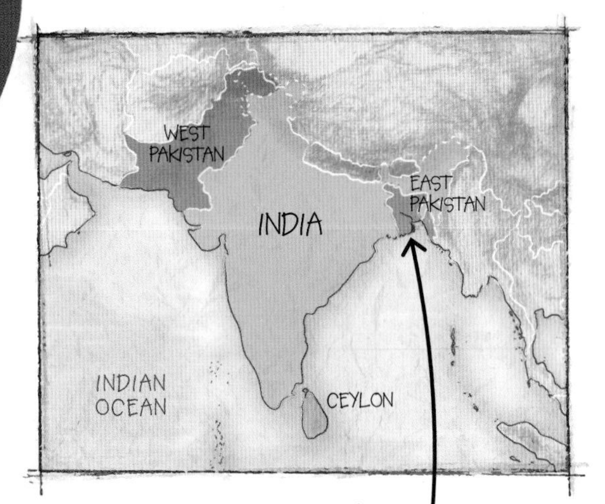

In 1971, East Pakistan became the independent country of Bangladesh.

He gave speeches sitting at a spinning wheel to encourage people to make their own clothes and to live a simple life.

The **14th Dalai Lama** *(1935–) is the spiritual leader of Tibet. He lives in exile in India and campaigns for* **TIBETAN INDEPENDENCE** *from China.*

Aung San Suu Kyi *(1945–) campaigns for* **DEMOCRACY** *in military-ruled Burma and has spent 15 of the last 20 years under house arrest.*

Deng Xiaoping

The Communist who REBELLED against Communism, and masterminded the economic future of China

By the way...
I became very unpopular when, in 1989, I ordered the army to kill students demonstrating for democracy in Tiananmen Square.

All about me

- **BORN:** 1904
- **DIED:** 1997
- **NATIONALITY:** Chinese
- **FACTOID:** My name is pronounced as "dung".
- **IN A NUTSHELL:** I discovered Marxism as a young man. I joined the Communist Party of China, but I didn't agree with the way that they ran the country.

Opening China to the world

Until the 19th century, China had been one of the **world's largest economies**. However, under Communist rule, the country was closed off from the rest of the world and, by the middle of the 20th century, it was struggling. Deng made ***economic reforms*** that allowed China to trade with the world again, which attracted foreign investment. Chinese students were also allowed to travel abroad to learn the latest **TECHNOLOGIES**.

Deng turned China's backward cities into modern economic powerhouses.

A mixed legacy

In just 20 years, under Deng's guidance, China went from being a ***backward farming nation*** to one of the world's largest economies. He **improved living standards** and gave citizens more freedom. However, to control the exploding population, he only allowed families to have **ONE CHILD**, which led to a lot of baby girls being abandoned because boys were seen to be more useful.

Mikhail Gorbachev

The Communist who killed off COMMUNISM in the USSR

All about me

- **BORN:** 1931
- **NATIONALITY:** Russian
- **FACTOID:** I graduated from the Moscow State University Law School in 1955.
- **ANOTHER FACTOID:** I won the Nobel Peace Prize in 1990.
- **IN A NUTSHELL:** I became general secretary of the Communist Party in 1985, and president of the USSR in 1988.

In 1989, the fall of the Berlin Wall, which divided East (communist) Berlin from West (democratic) Berlin, symbolized the end of the Cold War.

By the way... my reforms helped to bring the Cold War to an end and signalled the beginning of the end of the Communist Party in the USSR.

Communism before Gorbachev

The philospher Karl Marx (1818–1883) said that power should be in the hands of the people and **wealth should be shared equally**. In 1917, Vladimir Lenin (1870–1924) led the **RUSSIAN REVOLUTION** and, in 1922, Russia became the Union of Soviet Socialist Republics (USSR). Under ***Communist rule***, the USSR became closed off from the rest of the world and, by the time Gorbachev took over, its economy was in a mess.

The radical reformer

Gorbachev reformed the Soviet Union's economy, and **GAVE NEW FREEDOMS** to Soviet citizens. He opened up talks with Western democracies and, in 1987, he struck a deal with America to end the **nuclear arms race,** which signalled an end to the Cold War. The following year he ***withdrew Soviet control*** in the Eastern Bloc states in Europe, who then overthrew their Communist regimes.

Nelson Mandela

The man who gave AFRICA back to its people

Mandela fought long and hard against apartheid in South Africa, and spent 27 years in prison, before he was voted the country's first black president.

Young activist

Rolihlahla Mandela was born in Transkei, South Africa, in 1918, and was later given the name **Nelson** by his teacher. After he qualified as a lawyer he became involved with a group trying to bring about ***political change*** in South Africa, called the **AFRICAN NATIONAL CONGRESS (ANC).**

The fight for freedom

In 1948, the white South African government brought in "apartheid" laws that meant that white and black people had to stay **SEPARATE**. Mandela became deputy leader of the ANC, and they started peaceful protests. But, after police killed 69 protestors, the ANC became more ***violent***. The government banned the ANC and Mandela was **arrested** for plotting against the government. In 1964, he was sentenced to **LIFE IMPRISONMENT**.

He couldn't have done it without...

In prison, Mandela was inspired by **WILLIAM HENLEY'S** *(1849–1903) poem* **INVICTUS:** *"I am the master of my fate, I am the captain of my soul".*

South Africa's first black Archbishop **DESMOND TUTU** *(1931–) was, like Mandela, an extremely passionate anti-apartheid* **CAMPAIGNER.**

By the way...
my great-grandfather Ngubengcuka ruled as king of a South African tribe called the Thembu people.

MANDELA FOR PRESIDENT

THE PEOPLE'S CHOICE!

From prison to power

During his total of **27 years in prison**, Mandela became a symbol of resistance to apartheid around the world. In 1990, he was released, and the ban against the ANC was lifted. In 1991, Mandela became the ANC's leader. He was awarded the ***Nobel Peace Prize*** in 1993, and the following year South Africa held its first multi-racial election. Mandela was elected the first black **PRESIDENT**.

Mandela is one of the most awarded people in history, with more than 250 awards

National hero

Mandela fought for freedom for black South Africans and kept the peace when apartheid ended, even though many people wanted revenge against white land-owners. In 2009, the UN announced that Mandela's birthday, 18 July, would be "Mandela Day".

Mandela was inspired by Indian activist **MAHATMA GANDHI'S** *(1869–1948) "satyagraha" methods of* **NON-VIOLENT** *protest.*

WALTER SISULU *(1912–2003) and* **OLIVER TAMBO** *(1917–1993) were Mandela's fellow anti-apartheid activists, and* **ANC MEMBERS**.

Clued-up

Creatives

The world just wouldn't be the same without these rare talents who have brightened our lives with their creations. They have entertained us with their stories, art, games, music, fashion, and movies – even the package holiday. Thanks to them, boredom isn't an option.

Believe it or not, people were writing books long before Harry Potter came around. Some of them were pretty good, too.

William Shakespeare

(1564–1616)

School children all over the world might think this English writer is **BORING**, but with the likes of **Hamlet, Othello, King Lear, and Macbeth**, he created some of literature's ***greatest characters***. He was a real wordsmith, too, inventing around 1,700 of the words we use today.

Shakespeare's wife and children were all illiterate

Voltaire

(1694–1778)

This French writer just couldn't stop. He wrote more than ***2,000 books*** and pamphlets, and an incredible 20,000 letters. **He used his wit to criticize** the king and government, and spent most of his life in **FEAR OF BEING JAILED**.

Aleksandr Pushkin

(1799–1837)

Books in Russia were **pretty boring** until Pushkin came along and shook things up. He threw away the ***formal language style*** used before him and wrote his books in the sort of language people used in **EVERYDAY LIFE**. His work has influenced Russian literature ever since.

ushkin died at age 37 when he was defeated in a duel

Lu Xun

(1881–1936)

For centuries, Chinese stories always had a **god as the hero**. Lu Xun wrote his stories from the ***point of view of normal people***, which was far more engaging. He is known as the **FATHER OF MODERN CHINESE LITERATURE**.

Virginia Woolf

(1882–1941)

This English feminist author came up with a ***new kind of storytelling***. Her stories were told in the same way that people think – by using her character's **inner voice** to tell the tale through their thoughts in a **STREAM OF CONCIOUSNESS**.

Thomas Cook

The man who sent Britain PACKING

By the way... when I organized my first round-the-world tour, I travelled more than 40,000 km (25,000 miles), and was away for 222 days.

In the 1800s, a holiday was just an ice cream and a paddle at the nearest beach until Thomas Cook opened up the world.

Preaching to the people

Thomas Cook was born in Derbyshire, England, in 1808. He trained as a cabinet-maker, but was also very ***religious*** and spent his spare time with a local **TEMPERANCE SOCIETY** that travelled around telling people why they **shouldn't drink alcohol**.

Training for success

In 1841, Cook **arranged a trip** for 570 members of his temperance society on a new railway that had been built from Leicester to Loughborough. **HE CHARGED THE PASSENGERS** one shilling to cover the cost of the trip and lunch. ***The trip was a great success***, and Cook realized he was onto something.

Did you know? Cook wrote one of the first travel guides, *A Handbook of the Trip to Liverpool.*

He paved the way for...

A pioneer of package holidays, Russian entrepreneur **VLADIMIR RAITZ** *(1922–2010) was the first person to use* **CHARTER FLIGHTS.**

The Mayor of Benidorm, Spain, **PEDRO ZARAGOZA** *(1922–2008) turned the town into the first* **PACKAGE HOLIDAY RESORT.**

Cook invented the traveller's cheque in 1874

The Nile Voyage

THOS. COOK & SON OFFER YOU THE FINEST RIVER STEAMERS IN THE WORLD

Luxurious State-Rooms : Spacious Decks : Private Bath-Rooms
Unrivalled Comfort : Hot and cold running water in every cabin

THREE WEEKS' VOYAGE to LUXOR & ASWAN AND BACK
The S.S. "SUDAN," "ARABIA" & "EGYPT" leave Cairo weekly on Wednesdays from November 7th to March—FARE £70

TWO WEEKS' VOYAGE to LUXOR & ASWAN AND BACK
The S.S. "ROSETTA" & "DAMIETTA" leave Asyut weekly on Saturdays from January 5th to March — FARE £56
(including railway fare from Cairo to Asyut and return).

ONE WEEK'S VOYAGE to ABU-SIMBEL & HALFA AND BACK
The S.S. "THEBES" leaves Aswan (Shellal) weekly on Mondays in connection with both the above services—FARE £30

Apply to :—

THOS. COOK & SON LTD.

CHIEF OFFICE:—

BERKELEY ST., PICCADILLY, LONDON, W.1.

Branches at Cairo, Luxor, Aswan, Alexandria, Port Said, Khartoum and throughout the world.

Egypt 1922

"EGYPT AND THE SUDAN" *will be sent post free on application to:*— Egypt Enquiry Bureau, 3, Regent St., London, S.W.1; Tourist Development Association, Cairo Station, Cairo; or any of the prominent Travel Agencies.

Steaming forward

Cook started running **regular railway trips** and was soon conducting tours of Scotland. His trips grew in popularity and, by 1863, he had moved to London and was organizing tours to ***exotic locations like Egypt.*** By 1872, Thomas Cook was offering a **212-DAY ROUND-THE-WORLD TOUR**. For only 270 guineas, people could travel by steamship across the Atlantic, catch a stagecoach across America, and take a paddle steamer to Japan.

The world is your oyster

The idea of buying one ticket to cover an entire trip was revolutionary. Cook's package holidays made affordable travel available to ordinary citizens at a time when only the rich could afford such luxuries.

The **NO-FRILLS** *airline was pioneered in 1966 by* **FREDDIE LAKER** *(1922–2006). It made travel much more affordable.*

RICHARD BRANSON'S *(1950–)* **VIRGIN GALACTIC** *will be the first company to offer flights into space to members of the public.*

Walt Disney

The man who brought DRAWINGS to life

Walt Disney brought us some of the world's best-loved cartoon characters, making the world a more colourful and magical place.

Early sketches

Walt Disney was born in 1901 in Chicago, USA. From the age of four, he lived on a farm where he discovered his love of drawing animals. He won a **scholarship** to art college and, when he left, he started a company with his animator friend Ub Iwerks (1901–1971), making short **ANIMATED** films for a chain of theatres. Unfortunately, the company went bankrupt, so Walt and Ub ***moved to Hollywood***.

By the way... my character Mickey Mouse was originally called "Mortimer Mouse", but my wife thought "Mortimer" was too serious.

Did you know? Disney was nominated for 59 Oscars and he won 22 of them – more than anyone else in the world.

He couldn't have done it without...

William George Horner *(1786–1837) invented the modern* **ZOETROPE** *in 1834. It created the illusion that a drawing was moving.*

Spinning the cylinder and looking through the slits makes the sequence of images inside appear to move.

First feature

In 1934, Disney came up with the idea of creating a movie-length cartoon called *Snow White and the Seven Dwarfs*. Everyone in **Hollywood** thought it was a silly idea and joked about it being "Disney's Folly". However, *Snow White* was a **HUGE SUCCESS** and even won an Oscar. In 1946, Disney also pioneered mixed animation with live-action in *Song of the South*.

Disneyland

In 1955, Disney gave his creations a new home when he opened the "**DISNEYLAND**" theme park in California, USA. This brought together characters from his cartoons, films, and TV series. Disneyland soon became one of the world's most ***popular*** tourist attractions.

A colourful pioneer

Walt wasn't the first person to create animations, but he was the first to add sound and colour. His pioneering film techniques transformed the entertainment industry and put smiles on the faces of millions of people.

Flip books have one image on each sheet. Each image is slightly different to the previous one.

In 1868, **JOHN BARNES LINNETT** *invented the* **FLIP BOOK**. *When flipped quickly, the sequence of images fools your brain into seeing a moving image.*

In 1892, **CHARLES EMILE REYNAUD** *(1844–1918) projected the* **FIRST ANIMATED FILM,** *a loop of 500 hand-painted images, which lasted about 15 minutes.*

Gallery of artists

Ever since people first populated the planet, there have been artists who created beautiful imagery. These artists really made their mark.

Bringing more COLOUR to the world

Leonardo da Vinci

(1452–1519)

Italian **RENAISSANCE MAN** da Vinci was not content with creating some of art's greatest works, including the ***Mona Lisa*** and the ***Last Supper***, so he also studied anatomy, geology, gravity, optics, and flight. **He designed the first bicycle**, helicopter and parachute. He even created a robot knight!

Leonardo's ideas were well ahead of his time

Auguste Rodin

(1840–1917)

This French sculptor **wasn't afraid to show man's bad points**. His sculptures showed misery and weakness, as well as beauty and passion. Some of his most famous works, such as ***The Thinker*** and ***The Age of Bronze***, were **SO REALISTIC** that many people believed he had somehow cheated.

Rodin showed his subjects as they really appeared – even when he sculpted himself.

Vincent van Gogh
(1853–1890)

This tortured Dutch painter ***created all his work in just 10 years***. His paintings are known for their **BRIGHT COLOURS AND BOLD BRUSH STROKES**. Even though he is considered to be one of the greatest post-impressionist painters, **he lived in poverty**, and sold only one painting while he was alive.

After a fight, van Gogh cut off part of his ear

Pablo Picasso
(1881–1973)

Spanish artist Picasso was the playboy of the art world. He **experimented with lots of different styles**, but is best known for creating "**CUBISM**", which uses shapes such as triangles and squares to create an impression of the subject. Unlike van Gogh, Picasso had no trouble selling his paintings and ***became very rich***.

Frida Kahlo
(1907–1954)

Kahlo was a Mexican artist who mixed traditional Mexican art with modern "**SURREALISM**" (a strange dream-like style). After a bus crash left her crippled and in constant pain, she started creating oil paintings ***to distract herself***. Many of her paintings are self-portraits, which, despite their bright colours, **reflect her suffering**.

Coco Chanel

The woman who STYLED the 20th century, and changed the face of fashion

All about me

- **BORN:** 1883
- **DIED:** 1971
- **NATIONALITY:** French
- **FACTOID:** I lived in the Ritz hotel for more than 30 years.
- **IN A NUTSHELL:** My mother died of tuberculosis, and my father left the family, so I spent six years in an orphanage.

Chanel's clothes were custom-made using only the highest quality fabric.

Trendsetter

Coco opened her first shop in Paris, France, in 1909. At first she sold hats, but soon she started selling **luxury clothes**, fabrics, and jewellery. Coco introduced styles to the fashion world that were seen to be **RADICAL** at the time, such as the bobbed haircut, trousers for women, bathing suits, and the **little black dress**. She even (accidentally) made the sun tan fashionable when she got sunburned while on holiday.

By the way...
my real name was Gabrielle Bonheur Chanel. After I left the orphanage, I worked as a cabaret singer, where I became known as "Coco".

Chanel No 5 is still the world's bestselling perfume.

Going global

Coco's little fashion boutique became one of the most ***profitable and iconic*** fashion houses of all time. Her most famous product was a **perfume**, Chanel No 5, which made her one of the richest women in the world. Even today, she is regarded as an **ICON OF STYLE AND ELEGANCE**, and her classic designs still influence fashion.

N°5
CHANEL
EAU DE PARFUM

David Ogilvy

The man who created the idea of a BRAND and became the "father of modern advertising"

All about me

- **BORN:** 1911
- **DIED:** 1999
- **NATIONALITY:** English
- **FACTOID:** I was also a cook, a farmer, and a spy.
- **IN A NUTSHELL:** I started selling Aga cooking stoves door-to-door in Scotland. My big break came after I wrote a manual for other Aga salesmen on how to sell more ovens.

By the way... my book, *Confessions of an Advertising Man* became one of the most popular and famous books on advertising. It's still a bestseller.

A new approach

A big **advertising agency** were so impressed by David's Aga manual that they gave him a job as an ***account executive***. His first success came when he was put in charge of a hotel opening. He printed lots of postcards and sent them to everyone in the local phone book. The hotel opened to a **FULL HOUSE**.

Sales Manual

Ogilvy's Aga sales manual became an instant classic.

The slogan king

In 1948, Ogilvy started up his own advertising agency **Hewitt, Ogilvy, Benson, and Mather**. He created many of the world's most successful **ADVERTISING CAMPAIGNS**. He helped double Rolls-Royce sales with the slogan "At 60 miles an hour, the loudest noise in this new Rolls-Royce comes from the electric clock". Another huge success was his "Schweppervesence" campaign for the drinks manufacturer. Soon everyone was ***copying his style***.

Ole Kirk Kristiansen

The BRICK that changed the world

The LEGO® Group began with Ole Kirk Kristiansen's belief that "only the best is good enough". In time, a little plastic brick would take the world by storm.

Starting blocks

Kristiansen was born in the village of Filskov, Denmark, in 1891. When he finished school, he became a ***carpenter*** and started his own business. He built houses, and made stepladders and ironing boards, but **he also made toys**, including trains, cars, and ducks. In 1934, he named the company LEGO, deriving from two Danish words *leg godt*, or **PLAY WELL**.

By the way...
in 1949, I launched "Automatic Binding Bricks", but it wasn't until 1958 that my son, Godtfred Kirk Kristiansen, invented the LEGO brick as we know it today.

He couldn't have done it without...

The FIRST BUILDING BLOCK SET *was made of wood by the brilliant German educator* FRIEDRICH FROEBEL *(1782–1882) in 1840.*

American toymakers JESSE *(1858–1920) and* CHARLES CRANDALL *(1833–1905) made the first* INTERLOCKING *blocks in the 1860s.*

Building excitement

LEGO bricks could **LINK TOGETHER,** which meant children could build all sorts of exciting shapes. After the LEGO Group launched the brightly coloured plastic bricks, intensive work was carried out to improve the bricks. In 1955, the LEGO Group produced the "**LEGO System of Play**", focusing on the endless possibilities of the LEGO brick. They even brought out a ***version for smaller hands***, called LEGO® DUPLO®.

LEGO conquers the world

The first LEGO sets went on sale in America in 1961, and it wasn't long until they were **on sale throughout the world**. In 1977, they brought out kits for older kids called LEGO Technic. Today, you can buy sets that let you build your favourite vehicles and characters from blockbuster films, and even ***programmable robots***. People enjoy LEGO computer games, and can visit LEGOLAND **THEME PARKS**.

The number of LEGO bricks sold each year could reach five times around the world.

Building imaginations

LEGO bricks gave children a tool to be creative like no toy before or after it, and is still one of the world's most popular toys. In 60 years, the company has made an amazing 400 billion parts – that's 62 bricks for every person on the planet.

In 1882, **FRIEDRICH RICHTER** *(1847–1910) from Germany popularized* **ANCHOR BLOCKS**.

The **IVARSSON BROTHERS** *from Sweden founded* **BRIO** *in 1908, and made connecting wooden trains.*

Musicians

Making music from their IMAGINATIONS

A composer can turn a bunch of squiggles into music so powerful it casts a spell on you. Meet some masters of musical magic.

The piano was invented in Italy around 1700

Johann Sebastian Bach
(1685–1750)

As a child, Bach had a beautiful soprano voice. This German is considered to be one of the **GREATEST COMPOSERS** who ever lived, but, while he was alive, he was more famous as a great organist. It wasn't until he'd been dead for 100 years that his ***true genius*** was recognized.

Wolfgang Amadeus Mozart
(1756–1791)

The **PRECOCIOUS** young Austrian started composing music when he was just five years old. He ***toured the courts*** of Europe when he was just six, and, by the time he was an old man of 14, he had written his first opera.

Peter Ilyich Tchaikovsky
(1840–1893)

Russian composer Tchaikovsky began piano lessons when he was five and could **read music better than his dad** by the time he was eight. His ballet *The Nutcracker* is a winter holiday favourite, and *Swan Lake* remains popular.

Ali Akbar Khan
(1922–2009)

This Indian musician thought six-string guitars were for wimps, so he played an Indian version, called a **SAROD** that had 25 strings! He was the ***court musician for a Mahararaja,*** and was credited with bringing Indian music to attention of the world.

Toru Takematisu
(1930–1996)

This **SELF-TAUGHT** Japanese musician and composer brought together jazz, popular music, western classical music, and oriental music. He composed the score for more than ***90 Japanese films***, but is better known in the Western world as a classical composer.

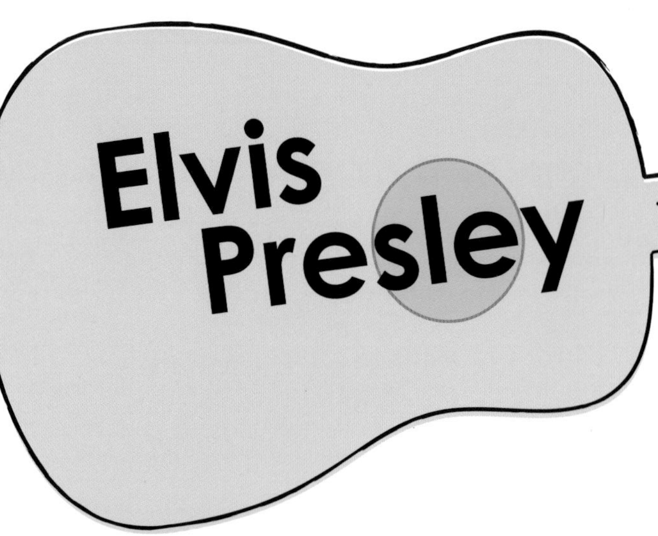

Elvis Presley

The KING of rock and roll

Elvis Presley was a singer, film star, and cultural icon. He starred in many films and sold more than a billion records – that's why fans call him the "king".

Young rocker

Elvis Aaron Presley was born, in Tupelo, Mississippi, USA, in 1935. When he was just a young boy he entered a **singing competition**, but came only fifth. For his tenth birthday he was given a **GUITAR**, even though he really wanted a bicycle. He soon started taking his guitar to school and would play and sing at lunchtime.

A new sound

His first single, "***That's alright***", was released in 1954. The first time it was played on the radio, the listeners loved it so much that the DJ played it again and again for two whole hours. His unique sound that he took from traditional blues music and his **hip-shaking** dance moves were unlike anything that people had ever heard or seen before. By the time Elvis died in 1977, he had sold more than **600 MILLION** singles and albums.

He paved the way for...

With songs like "Johnny be Good" and "Roll over Beethoven", **CHUCK BERRY** *(1926–) was a pioneer of rock and roll music in the 1950s.*

Uh-hu-ha. Yes m'am.

Military green to silver screen

By 1956, Elvis was appearing on the radio, TV, and in films. In 1957, he was drafted into the US army and, when he came back, he starred in a film called ***GI Blues***. He starred in **33 FILMS** and made history with his television appearances and **record-breaking** live concerts.

Top of the pops

Elvis may have done more to change American popular culture than anyone else. His music paved the way for more black musicians to become popular. Millions of fans visit "Graceland", his home in Memphis, USA.

By the way...

My gyrating hip moves earned me the nickname "Elvis the Pelvis". This move was thought to be "too much" for TV, and cameras were only allowed to film me from the hips up!

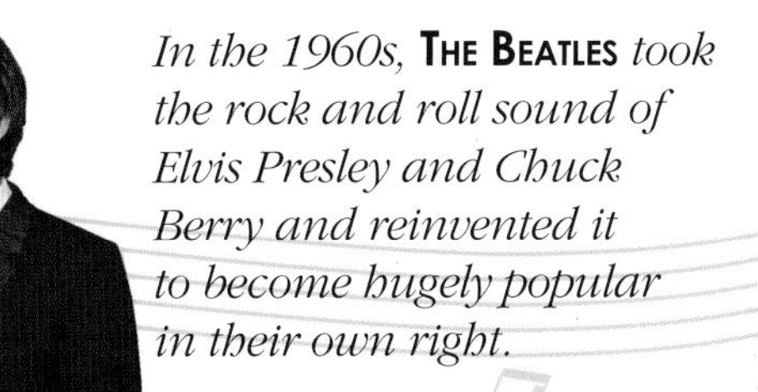

In the 1960s, **THE BEATLES** *took the rock and roll sound of Elvis Presley and Chuck Berry and reinvented it to become hugely popular in their own right.*

You don't have to look far to find an **ELVIS IMPERSONATOR**. *Today, more than 100,000 people around the world make a living by impersonating him.*

Let's applaud...

They may not have made the top 100 – but these TOP PEOPLE made a top contribution to BRITISH HISTORY.

Boudicca (c.30–60)
In 60 CE, the fiery warrior queen of the Celtic Iceni people led a major uprising against the occupying Roman forces, and tried – but failed – to kick them out of Britain.

William the Conquerer (c. 1028–1087)
In 1066, the Duke of Normandy defeated the last Anglo-Saxon king of England. He was crowned king and brought a bit of French *Je ne sais quoi* to England's culture, politics, and language.

Geoffrey Chaucer (c.1343–1400)
Geoffrey Chaucer's popular poems, including *The Canterbury Tales*, helped to legitimize the written English language. Otherwise you might be reading this book in French or Latin!

Elizabeth I (1533–1603)
Back in the good old days, we had Queen Bess. Her Elizabethan era was a golden age in English history, which included the defeat of the Spanish Armada in 1588.

Sir Walter Raleigh (1554–1618)
The favourite explorer of Queen Elizabeth I, Raleigh sailed to America and sponsored the first colony there. It didn't last long, but he did bring back potatoes. Imagine life without them...

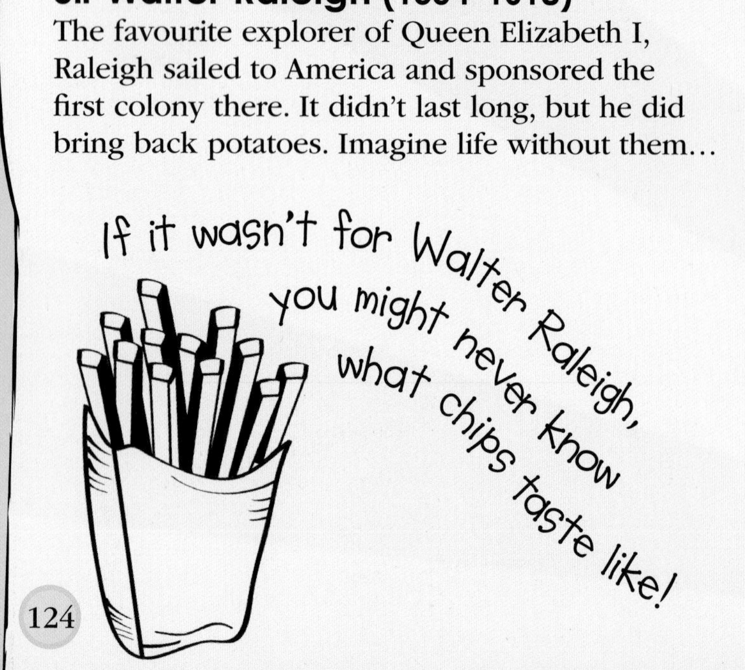

Francis Bacon (1561–1626)
Science used to be all talk, and clever men just debated ideas to discover the truth. However, Bacon argued that science needed to be proved by finding evidence in the real world.

Oliver Cromwell (1599–1658)
In 1649, Charles I was overthrown in the English Civil War. The king got the chop, and the political and military leader Cromwell ruled England as a republic from 1653 to 1658.

Sir Christopher Wren (1632–1723)
When the Great Fire of London burnt London to a crisp in 1666, the architect Christopher Wren redesigned the new St Paul's Cathedral and many churches that are still standing today.

Adam Smith (1723–1790)
The Scottish philosopher Adam Smith is considered the father of modern economics and Capitalism. He argued that a free market results in the greatest good for society overall.

Captain James Cook (1728–1779)
Captain Cook was the first European to make it Down Under. Stopping off at Hawaii and New Zealand on the way, he landed on the east coast of Australia in 1770, and formed a colony there.

Sir Richard Arkwright (1732–1792)
Wigmaker Richard Arkwright took up inventing when wigs went out of fashion. Turns out he was quite good at it – his spinning machines were crucial to the Industrial Revolution.

Olaudah Equiano (1745–1797)
Enslaved as a child in Africa, Olaudah went on to buy his freedom and became one of the most important figures in the British movement towards the abolition of slavery.

sambard Kingdom Brunel (1806–1859)

master at engineering, Brunel revolutionized ublic transport in the Victorian era with fantastic ridges, ships, tunnels, and Britain's first ever najor railway.

Charles Dickens (1812–1870)

n his novels Dickens brought attention to various ocial problems, such as poverty, and created many olourful characters, including Scrooge, the Artful Dodger, and Oliver Twist.

John Snow (1813–1858)

n 1854, John Snow tracked down the source of he deadly disease, cholera. People thought they aught it from breathing "bad air", but he proved hat it was down to drinking dirty water.

David Livingstone (1813–1873)

Scottish missionary and doctor, David ivingstone was one of the greatest European xplorers of Africa in the nineteenth century, nd publicized the horrors of the slave trade.

Joseph Bazalgette (1819–1891)

oseph Bazalgette was the engineer who created ondon's first sewer network in the 1860s. It elieved the city from cholera epidemics and ots of disgusting sights and smells!

James Starley (1831–1871)

James Starley put the bicycle industry into gear. His innovative inventions, which included gears, metal spokes, and chains, developed the modern bike, and we have been pedalling away ever since.

The Penny Farthing was the first machine to be called a "bicycle"

Mrs Beeton (1836–1865)

Mrs Beeton was the original domestic goddess. n 1861, she wrote *Mrs Beeton's Book of Household Management*, which became one of the most uccessful cookery books published.

Elizabeth Garrett-Anderson (1836–1917)

Elizabeth fought against prejudice to become England's first qualified female doctor. She founded the New Hospital for Women in London and paved the way for other female doctors.

Howard Carter (1874–1939)

Howard Carter dug his way to fame. In 1922, he discovered the tomb of Tutankhamun – the best preserved pharaoh's tomb ever found – in the Valley of the Kings, Egypt.

Tutankhamun was just a boy when he ascended to the throne, in 1333 BCE

Sir Winston Churchill (1874–1965)

Referred to as the "British Bulldog", Churchill was the prime minister of Great Britain from 1940 to 1945, leading the country to victory during the Second World War, and becoming a national hero.

William Beveridge (1879–1963)

This economist outlined the welfare state that was introduced by the Labour government after the Second World War. This gave free medical treatment for all, and benefit payments for the poor.

James Goodfellow (1937–)

James Goodfellow invented the Automated Teller Machine (ATM) and Personal Identification Numbers (PINs) in the 1960s, so now people can withdraw money at any time.

Stephen Hawking (1942–)

Hawking is a physicist and cosmologist whose books and public appearances have introduced tricky subjects, such as black holes and the Big Bang theory, to the general public.

JK Rowling (1965–)

Rowling unleashed a publishing phenomenon and an obsession with wizards with her Harry Potter books, entertaining millions of children (and adults) around the world.

Glossary

Antibiotic
A medical drug that kills or slows down the growth of bacteria and other micro-organisms.

Antiseptic
A substance that prevents the growth of organisms that can cause disease.

Apartheid
A policy of racial segregation that was enforced by the South African government from 1948 to 1994.

Archaeology
The study of history through analysis of excavation sites and remains.

Astronomy
The study of science that relates to space, the planets, and the Universe.

Bacteria
Single-celled micro-organisms, some of which can cause diseases.

Binary code
A system that uses the digits 1 and 0 to represent a number, letter, or character.

Bolsheviks
A faction within the Russian Social Democratic Party, which later became the Communist party in 1918.

Browser
A computer program that allows people to find, view, and navigate between different websites or web pages.

Chemistry
The study of science that relates to substances, and the way they interact, change, and combine.

Civil rights
The rights of citizens to be socially and politically equal.

Cold War
Period of hostility (1946–1991) between communist nations (led by the Soviet Union) and capitalist nations (led by the USA) that stopped short of actual war.

Colony
A territory under political control of another country, usually occupied by settlers from that country.

Communism
A system of government in which the state controls the economy, and goods are equally shared.

Constitution
A set of laws or rules that determine the political principles of a government.

Democracy
A government elected by the people.

Element
A substance in which all the atoms are the same, and cannot be broken down by another substance.

Empire
A group of countries under single political or military rule.

Enlightenment (Buddhism)
The state of spiritual knowledge, which frees a person from the cycle of rebirth.

Entrepreneur
An individual who takes on a financial risk to run a business.

Evolution
The theory of how species adapt to their surroundings over a long time.

Fossil
The remains of past animal or plant life found in rocks.

Genetics
A branch of biology that explores heredity and how traits are passed on through generations.

Heresy
The act of holding opinions that go against the teachings of the church.

Martyr
A person who is killed for refusing to renounce their religious beliefs.

Mecca
This city is in modern-day Saudi Arabia and is the spiritual centre of Islam.

Microchip
A computer component used to carry out a range of electronic functions.

Morality
Beliefs based on the principles of what is right and wrong.

Patent
The exclusive rights held by an invento or company to make use of a specific process or invention.

Physics
The study of science relating primarily to energy and matter.

Psychology
The scientific study of the mind and how it relates to human behaviour.

Renaissance
A period from the 14th to 16th centurie in Europe when there was a surge of interest in the arts and sciences.

Revolution
Overthrowing a government or politica system, usually with force.

Saint
A person recognized by the church as being exceptionally virtuous.

Server
A computer, or software on a computer, providing services to other computers that connect to it over a network.

Suffrage
The right to vote in a political election.

Vaccination
Precautionary medical treatment that stops you contracting a disease.

World Wide Web
An interconnected set of hyperlinked documents spread throughout the Internet.

Index

Acknowledgements

DK WOULD LIKE TO THANK:
Ed Merritt for creating maps. Liz Moore for additional picture research. Jackie Brind for the index and Carron Brown for proofreading. All the people at the LEGO Group and Sarah Harland at DK for their help with the "Ole Kirk Kristiansen" spread, and Professor Denise Cush for her insightful comments relating to the "Religious leaders" spread.

THE PUBLISHER WOULD LIKE TO THANK THE FOLLOWING FOR THEIR KIND PERMISSION TO REPRODUCE THEIR PHOTOGRAPHS:
Key: a–above; b–below/bottom; c–centre; f–far; l–left; r–right; t–top

akg-images: 32tr; **Alamy Images:** Ancient Art & Architecture Collection Ltd / Kadokawa 89bc; Archive Pics 49tr, 51cla; Art Directors & TRIP 60br; The Art Gallery Collection 18br, 72fbl, 84-85b; Pat Behnke 119tr; Matthew Chattle 118cr; GL Archive 87cl; Tim Graham 64tr, 64cl; Interfoto 82clb, 93br, 118bl; James Osmond Photography 82bl; Jeff Morgan 13 117br; Michael Jenner 82br; Mark LaMoyne 117fcl; Lebrecht Music and Arts Photo Library 17bl, 72br; Lordprice Collection 58bl; Mary Evans Picture Library 59tl, 65cr, 83br, 86br, 91c; Moviestore Collection Ltd. / Disney SSNW 010FOH 113tc; Nitschkefoto 118clb, 118cb, 118fcr, 119clb; North Wind Picture Archives 33cr, 33bc, 82tr, 83bl, 90tr, 92bl; Christine Osborne / World Religions Photo Library 71br; Photo Researchers 19bc; Photos 12 / Oasis 97bl; Pictorial Press Ltd 52br, 121cr; Maurice Savage 119crb; Robert Stainforth 83cra; Stella / Imagebroker 119cl; stu49 53bl; Gary Woods 117c (oven); World History Archive 13crb, 36cra, 37cr, 85tl, 85clb. **The Art Archive:** 46ca; Biblioteca Nazionale Marciana Venice / Gianni Dagli Orti 84cl; Bibliothèque Nationale Paris 89cl. **Atticpaper.com:** 118br. **benidormytu.com:** 110br. **The Bridgeman Art Library:** Galleria degli Uffizi, Florence, Italy 114tl; Mentz, Albrecht (15th century) (after) / Bibliotheque Nationale, Paris, France 33c; Museo Archeologico Nazionale, Naples, Italy / Giraudon 80cr; Private Collection 28cra, 97cl; Private Collection / Look and Learn 34c; Private Collection / The Stapleton Collection 67tc; The Stapleton Collection 86c; Private Collection / Ken Welsh 81cb. **CERN :** 54tr. **Corbis:** 3, 17tl, 21cl, 35cra, 59br, 103bl; Henny Ray Abrams / Reuters 111br; Albright-Knox Art Gallery 115br; Bettmann 12cl, 19tl, 21tl, 21cr, 22cra, 24cl, 25tl, 38tr, 48bl (orville), 48bl (wilbur), 48br, 49tl, 49tc, 58br, 63clb, 63fcla (freud), 73bc, 76clb, 82-83c, 98br, 99tr, 99bl, 99br, 109cl; Stefano Bianchetti 61cr, 85cra; Car Culture 50tr, 50c, 50ftr, 50-51c, 51tl, 51tl (convertible), 51tc, 51ftl; China Photos / Reuters 102br; Dean Conger 89br; Alfredo Dagli Orti / The Art Archive 91br; Pascal Deloche / Godong 70br; DLILLC 77tr; EPA / Everett Kennedy Brown 75cl; The Gallery Collection 20br, 88cra; Lynn Goldsmith 122bc; Heritage Images 19tr; Heritage Images / Ann Ronan Picture Library 108c; Yves Herman / Reuters 43tr; Hulton-Deutsch Collection 72-73cb; Jon Hursa / EPA 105cla; Kim Kulish 55tl; Lebrecht Authors / Lebrecht Music & Arts 109tr; Lebrecht Music & Arts 98cl; Lester Lefkowitz 43bc; Barry Lewis / In Pictures 88tr; Library of Congress - digital version / Science Faction 48cl; John Marian / Transtock 117cl; Michael Ochs Archives 122cla, 123cla, 123bl; Newton / PoodlesRock 15tl; Michael Nicholson 62br, 95bl; Richard T. Nowitz 123br; Ocean 25br; PoodlesRock 85bl; The Print Collector 99tl; Reuters / Apichart Weerawong 75tr; Reuters / Paul Yeung 102tl; Flip Schulke 69cl; Stapleton Collection 58cr; Jim Sugar 111bl; Sunset Boulevard 122crb; Swim Ink 62tl; Swim Ink 2, LLC 95cr; Frank Trapper 104br; David Turnley 104clb; Peter Turnley 103tr; Penny Tweedie 77cl; Underwood & Underwood 73tr, 116tl; Ivan Vdovin / JAI 91bl; Kimberly White / Reuters 52c; Adrianna Williams 53cl (iphone). **Dorling Kindersley:** The British Museum 88c, 88crb, 88fcrb, 89fcl; The Science Museum 52bl; The Science Museum, London 35c, 36br (voltaic pile), 41c, 46cb. **Dreamstime.com:** 74tl, 74tc, 74c; Petrisor Adrian 76bl, 76fbr, 77fbr; Alohashaka82 29c, 29bl, 29fcrb; Andrey Armyagov 76cr (clothing); Badlatitude 66cr;Gary Bass 112bl; Raynald Bélanger 66-67b, 67cb; William Berry 47cl (popcorn); Cammeraydave 74cr (wood); Gino Crescoli 11crb; Deckard73 117c (book); Dedmazay 125fcra; Evgeny Dubinchuk 14cb; Henri Faure 74cr (chair); Michael Flippo 68cr (3rd mic); Frenta 70-71; Martin Haas 68cr (2nd mic); I3alda 27cr; Joingate 46tc, 46cla, 46c (background), 46ftl; Ke77kz 89crb; Sabri Deniz Kizil 10fbl; Jacques Kloppers 75crb (sandals); Konstanttin 96-97c (scroll); Jakub Kostal 76cr (camera); Krakus324 66-67 (arrows); Connie Larsen 112cb; Olga Lyubkin 14cl (apple); Olira 117clb; Mohamed Osama 68cr (wood); Riccardo Perrone 96-97c (map); Ragnarock 29cra; Rambleon 101c; Rceeh 68cr (4th mic); Relato 68bl; Samy .g 75tl, 75bc, 75br; Sjgh 47tc, 47tr, 47cra, 47c; Sofiaworld 75cr (pattern); Jeremy Swinborne 47cl (tv); Maciej Szubert 67tl; Milos Tasic 14cl (chair); Christophe Testi 112cr (pencil); Timurock 116c (background), 116bl, 116bc; Andrzej Tokarski 29fcr; Gianni Tonazzini 113cl; Yael Weiss 27bl (magnifying glass); Kevin Woodrow 29cr; Yarmalade 100bl, 101bl, 101br; Yinghua 100crb; Zabiamdeve 113crb; Zash 26cb. **Flickr:** 7E55E-BRN 53tc. **Fotolia:** 3d world 86c (frame), 87tr (frame), 87br (frame); Algol 90fcr; Alperium 8crb; Apops 33clb; Auris 24cra; Beboy 23bl; Bloomua 52c (tablet); Franck Boston 55cra; Gregor Buir 52-53b (background); Derya Celik 80tl; HD Connelly 4-5 (light bulb), 30-31, 38tc (bulb), 41tc, 41tr, 41c (background), 41ftl; Danussa 61cl (fish), 61clb; Designer_Andrea 100-101c; Devilpup 36br (hands); Jamalludin din 8clb (kites); Lev Dolgatsjov 63fcla; Electriceye 123tl; Emily2k 38tl; Enens 62cl; Extezy 108bl; Fakegraphic 4-5 (ship); Igor Fjodorov 39cl; Paul Fleet 23tr, 37br; Google 65clb; Kheng Guan Toh 45bl; Hallgerd 111tl; Heywoody 93cl; Hfng 102cl, 102fcl; Adrian Hillman 104-105b; iNNOCENt 63br (cat); Irochka 61tl (scroll); Kalim 18cl (frame); Kayros Studio 63b (sofa); Andrey Kiselev 36br (body); Kjolak 80cla; Klipart.pl 45cl; Georgios Kollidas 123crb; Dariusz Kopestynski 9cr; Ralf Kraft 8cr; LaCatrina 52-53c (button); Paul Laroque 22bl, 43c; Lazypit 112t, 113t; Leks_052 82cr; Leremy 124bl; Lineartestpilot 44cr; Luminis 49bl; Magann 91cr; Anatoly Maslennikov 63cla, 63ca; Mircea Maties 81cra; Bram J. Meijer 8cb (fireworks); Mipan 22clb, 34ftr, 110crb, 111c; Alexandr Mitiuc 23br; MM 32cr; Igor Nazarenko 98tl; Ooz 4-5 (brain), 23cb, 56-57; Patrimonio Designs 44bl; Andrejs Pidjass 80cra (arm), 80c (arm); Regisser.com 32fcr; Rixx 108c (frame), 108br (frame), 109tr (frame), 109cl (frame), 109br (frame); Rolffimages 92tr; Sabphoto 37fcrb; Sellingpix 85clb (grass); Silavsale 68cr (podium); Alexander Spegalskiy 90crb; StarJumper 22-23t; Statsenko 22br; Sandra van der Steen 13fcla, 60cr (hand); James Steidl 99cl; Studiogriffon.com 82-83b; Stephen Sweet 49br; John Takai 61tl (whale), 81fcrb; Tombaky 25c (background); Tomislav 68cr (1st mic); Valdis Torms 25clb, 38tc (pin), 38clb, 39cb, 39ftr, Tomasz Trojanowski 53cl (body); Unpict 12fcra, 13cla; Pavlo Vakhrushev 8cb; Rui Vale de Sousa 52cr; Sergey Vasiliev 37cb (hand); Vege 98tr; Vlorzor 33cl; Slavcho Vradjev 8bc; VRD 8clb, wenani 98-99b; Bertold Werkmann 86br (frame), 87cl (frame). **fotoLibra :** Ime Udoma Ufot 45tl. **Getty Images:** AFP 69tr; AFP Photo / Walter Dhladhla 100br; Apic / Hulton Archive 17br, 23tl, 24tr, 60clb, 65bl, 97tr, 104c, 120cl; Archive Photos 116cl (blouse); Archive Photos / Stringer 80bc; Erich Auerbach / Hulton Archive 121clb; Bachrach / Archive Photos 45cr; Mathew Brady / Archive Photos 68br; The Bridgeman Art Library / After Nicholas de Largilliere 108br; The Bridgeman Art Library / Antoine Jean Gros 96cl; The Bridgeman Art Library / French School 90cl; The Bridgeman Art Library / Gaston Melingue 20cl; The Bridgeman Art Library / Vincent van Gogh 115tr; Central Press / Hulton Archive 26cra; China Span / Keren Su 58cra; Don Cravens / Time & Life Pictures 69bl; G. Dagli Orti / De Agostini 91tr; DEA / Veneranda Biblioteca Ambrosiana 84bl; Walter Dhladhla / AFP 105tr; Digital Vision 15bc; Digital Vision / Alexander Hassenstein 13clb; Emmanuel Dunand / AFP 101fbr; Evening Standard / Hulton Archive 67br; Express 26ca; Silvio Fiore 8tr; Flickr / Roevin 90bl; Fotosearch 38bl; Bill Hogan / Chicago Tribune / MCT 116br; Hulton Archive 11br, 12br, 16br, 18cl (ship), 19bl, 26bl, 42br, 44br, 47tl, 61br, 66br, 67bl, 81bc, 81br, 92cl, 92cr, 96bc; Hulton Archive / Archive Photos 1bl, 10fbr, 10-11, 41tl, 112cr (body); Imagno 80br; Imagno / Hulton Archive 11bc, 14br, 96cr; Kean Collection 96cra; Kean Collection / Hulton Archive 61bl; Keystone Features / Hulton Archive 13bl; Keystone-France / Gamma-Keystone 72-73ca; Alvin Langdon Coburn / George Eastman House / Archive Photos 76br; Leemage / Universal Images Group 92br Frederic Lewis 39bl; David Livingston 53tl; Francois Lochon / Gamma-Rapho 64br; Lonely Planet Images / Anders Blomqvist 70cl; Steve McAlister 32cl; Michael Ochs Archives 68tr; MIXA 40cr, 112cr (legs); Museum of the City of New York / Byron Collection 41bl; National Geographic / Michael Poliza 76crb; New York Daily News Archive 101tr; OFF / AFP 68cr (body); OJO Images 47cl (trousers); Photographer's Choice / Ian McKinnell 15c (planets); Photographer's Choice / Peter Dazeley 27bl (dna); PhotoQuest 51tr; Photosindia 64cr; Popperfoto 14cla, 67cr, 112tr; Andreas Rentz 54cl; Science Faction / Library of Congress 39tr; J. Shearer / WireImage 76tr; Howard Sochurek / Time & Life Pictures 58cl; SSPL 12clb, 14bc, 34bc, 35bl, 40c, 43tl, 44cl, 47cr, 53br, 112br, 113br; SSPL / Hulton Archive 47bl; Stock Montage 46tr, 74tr, 93bl; Stock Montage / Archive Photos 1cb, 11cl; Stone / Microzoa 74cr (body); Justin Sullivan 52tr; SuperStock 93tl, 93cra, 99cla, 120crb; Bob Thomas / Popperfoto 10bc; Time & Life Pictures / Howard Sochurek 100bc; Time & Life Pictures / Loomis Dean 67cl; Time & Life Pictures / Mansell 13br, 40bl, 69bc, 100cr; Time & Life Pictures / Neil Selkirk 77br; Time & Life Pictures / Stan Wayman 68clb; Time & Life Pictures / Wallace Kirkland 100tr; Tom Stoddart Archive / Hulton Archive 101bc; Universal History Archive / Hulton Archive 1cb (head), 10br, 11tl, 12cr, 13tl, 14cl (body), 15clb, 24br, 26cr, 40tr, 42cl, 42crb, 46cr, 53tr, 60bl, 66clb, 67fcla, 87br, 96br, 97br; Universal Images Group / Leemage 84bc, 85br. **NASA and The Hubble Heritage Team (AURA/ STScI):** 15br. **The Kobal Collection:** Paramount 123tr. **Mary Evans Picture Library:** 65cl. **The Natural History Museum, London:** 28bl. **The Nobel Foundation:** 42bl. **Press Association Images:** Polfoto 118tr. **Rex Features:** Everett Collection 117tl. **Peter Sanders:** 71tl. **Photo Scala, Florence:** White Images 88bc. **Science Photo Library:** 32br; Des Bartlett 29tr; John Reader 29clb; Science Source 27tc; Paul D. Stewart 28cl; Barbara Strnadova 29ca; Sheila Terry 34tr. **SuperStock:** 11tr; Bridgeman Art Library 115cl; Fotosearch 86br. **Thomas Cook Archives:** 110cl, 111tr. **TopFoto.co.uk:** 73c, 111cla; AP 105br; UPP 110bl. **U.S.F.W.S:** 77bc. **Wikipedia:** 12bl, 16bl, 18bl, 26bc, 48c, 50bl, 50br, 51br, 59bl, 72bl, 73bl, 87tr, 88br, 97crb, 104bl, 105bl, 109br, 121tl; Thenobleageofsteam 119bl.

JACKET CREDITS
FRONT: Alamy Images: Archive Pics bc (ford). **Corbis:** Bettmann fcra, ftr (orville), ftr (wilbur), ca; Car Culture bc (car); The Gallery Collection fcla; Heritage Images / Ann Ronan Picture Library fclb; Jon Hursa / EPA cra; Robbie Jack fbl; Barry Lewis / In Pictures fcla (helmet). **Dorling Kindersley:** The British Museum fcl (boots), fcl (knife). **Getty Images:** Apic / Hulton Archive br; Imagno / Hulton Archive bc (catherine); Time & Life Pictures / Wallace Kirkland tc. **BACK: Corbis:** Shift Foto fcla. **Fotolia:** Auris cr (flask). **Getty Images:** Apic / Hulton Archive cr; Central Press / Hulton Archive ftr; Hulton Archive br; Hulton Archive / Imagno tl; Keystone-France / Gamma-Keystone clb; Photodisc / ICHIRO fcl; Stone / Yann Layma cl; Universal History Archive / Hulton Archive tr. **SPINE: Getty Images:** Apic / Hulton Archive t. **ENDPAPERS: Fotolia:** HD Connelly (light bulb); Fakegraphic (ship); Ooz (brain).